prosple

Prosple is a one-stop career platform for students seeking jobs and internships. Our curated opportunities are hand-picked for students (i.e. no '3+ years of experience' nonsense!), and since 2014, we've helped over 23 million students on their career journeys.

Founded in Australia, we're a 100% remote team with members scattered around the world - New Zealand, the Philippines, Indonesia, France, Norway, and beyond.

START EXPLORING THOUSANDS OF INTERNSHIPS AND GRADUATE JOBS

Scan to get started

![prosple]

Published by: Prosple Pty Ltd

Creative production:
Jeffrey Duncan
Yohanne Zapata-Esguerra

Writing and editing:
Frances Chan
Lovely Barba-Aquino
Naomi Ndifon

Layout and design:
Patricia Anne Bellido
Amelia Paycana Espaldon
John Paulo Fernandez
Francheska May Dante

Advertising:
Geoff Adams
geoff.adams@prosple.com
+61 467 777 079

Grant Robson
grant.robson@prosple.com
+61 492 471 319

au.prosple.com
contact@prosple.com

ISBN: 978-0-6484930-6-8
ISSN: 2204-471X

Volume 7, May 2024

©**Prosple Pty Ltd**, May 2024

Table of contents

Hey there 04

Section 1

The Top 100 rankings 07
Find out the best companies and organisations hiring graduates
like yourself.

Section 2

What can you do with your degree? 25
Find out what students with your degree are doing in the 'real world'.

Section 3

What sectors can you work in? 39
Take a tour of the job market to discover what each sector is like and
which entry-level jobs you qualify for.

Accounting & advisory...40
Banking, trading & financial services...46
Construction & property services...52
Defence, R&D & manufacturing..58
Engineering consulting..64
Government & public service...70
Law...76
Management consulting...82
Mining, energy, oil & gas...88
Retail & consumer goods...94
Technology... 100

Section 4

How to get hired 107
Tips, tricks, and the inside scoop on how to land your dream role.

Your guide to a great career fair 108
7 tips for getting an internship 111
How to craft a winning CV.. 114
Your ultimate guide to psychometric tests 120
How to get an employee referral 124
How to ace interviews with the STAR technique 127

Section 5

Australia's Top 100 Graduate Employers......................133
Get a peek into life at these leading employers through exclusive
interviews, reviews, and more.

Hey there!

If you feel lost about your path after graduation or unsure about where to apply, you're not alone!

Every year, we as a society ask students to make one of the biggest decisions of their lives – while providing zero guidance along the way.

You know what we're talking about.

Those online quizzes telling you to be a crypto investor based on your horoscope.

Motivational posts on social media that say things like 'hustle hard and you'll be a #bossbabe in no time!'

The well-meaning tips from your step-cousin's great-aunt ('Just walk into a business and hand them your CV').

Ugh. No thanks.

That's where we come in

At Prosple, our approach is simple. We go out and ask recent grads about their jobs. What do they do all day, whether they like it, how they landed the gig in the first place – you get the gist.

We do this through interviews and extensive surveys. No zodiac signs. Just stories and experiences – real ones – giving you a genuine peek into different career paths.

So consider this book your career exploration companion. A collection of all the truths we've unearthed from those who were once standing where you are now.

Students waiting in line at a career fair, reading the Top 100 Graduate Employers book

How to use this book

If you don't know what you want to do yet, you can use this book to figure that out.

- Start with the 'What can you do with your degree?' section, which show what students from different academic backgrounds do in the real world. Find out what careers and companies align with your studies.

- Then let the 'What sectors can you work in?' section take you on a tour of the job market. You'll get the low-down on each industry and the specific entry-level roles companies are looking to fill.

Throughout the book, read first-hand accounts from people who work at the top companies. Learn about their daily grind and sample different careers through their experiences.

Survey the landscape and get a feel for all your options. Then, see what speaks to you, what sparks your interest.

If you already have a dream career in mind, use this book to fine-tune your search.

- Dive right into the Top 100 employers ranking and shortlist some companies that interest you. Scan their QR codes to see their ratings, reviews, and more.

- Check the 'How to get hired' section for our best tips on impressing employers from application to interview.

Then once you're ready, apply away!

> **Hint:** Make an account on Prosple to receive notifications when your favourite employers post jobs and internships.

Now go get 'em!

This book is full of real-world insights and opportunities, so take some time to explore, reflect, and let all the options sink in.

But remember: all the best advice in the world won't act on itself. So once you're armed with enough knowledge, swallow any self-doubt and take a confident first step into the real world.

We're rooting for you!

– The team at Prosple

Top 100 Employers

Good news!

Employers are hiring students and grads from all backgrounds! Check the key below to see who's recruiting students like you.

Key for relevant degrees:

B Business & Management	**E** Engineering & Mathematics	**I** IT & Computer Science
C Creative Arts	**H** Humanities, Arts & Social Sciences	**L** Law, Legal Studies & Justice

M Medical & Health Sciences	**S** Sciences
P Property & Built Environment	**T** Teaching & Education

Rank	Employer	Location of opportunities	Accepting applications from / Types of opportunities	Learn more
#1	**Capgemini Australia and New Zealand** **4.8** ★★★★★ #1 in Management consulting	⊙ Sydney, Melbourne, Brisbane, Adelaide, Hobart, Canberra, Auckland, Wellington, Christchurch	B C E H I L M P S T Graduate jobs Internships	Page 134
#2	**NAB Australia** **4.6** ★★★★★ #1 in Banking & financial services	⊙ All over Australia, work from home	B C E H I L M P S T Graduate jobs Internships	Page 134
#3	**Deloitte Australia** **4.2** ★★★★☆ #1 in Accounting & advisory	⊙ Sydney, Western Sydney, Melbourne, Perth, Brisbane, Adelaide, Canberra, Hobart, Launceston, Darwin	B C E H I L M P S T Graduate jobs Internships	Page 135
#4	**Commonwealth Bank** **4.4** ★★★★☆ #2 in Banking & financial servicess	⊙ Multiple locations in Australia	B C E H I L M P S T Graduate jobs Internships	Page 135

Key for relevant degrees:

B Business & Management	**C** Creative Arts	**E** Engineering & Mathematics
H Humanities, Arts & Social Sciences	**I** IT & Computer Science	

Rank	Employer		Location of opportunities	Accepting applications from / Types of opportunities	Learn more
#5	Optiver △	**Optiver** `4.5` ★★★★½ #1 in Trading	📍 Sydney	B E I S **Graduate jobs** **Internships**	Page 136
#6	Canva	**Canva** `4.3` ★★★★☆ #1 in Technology	📍 Sydney	B C E H I L M P S T **Graduate jobs** **Internships**	Page 136
#7	pwc	**PwC Australia** `3.7` ★★★½☆ #2 in Accounting & advisory	📍 Australia	B C E H I L M P S T **Graduate jobs** **Internships**	Page 137
#8		**Oliver Wyman Australia & New Zealand** `4.0` ★★★★☆ #2 in Management consulting	📍 Melbourne, Perth, Sydney	B C E H I L M P S T **Graduate jobs** **Internships**	Page 137
#9	ARUP	**Arup** `4.7` ★★★★★ #1 in Engineering consulting	📍 Adelaide, Canberra, Melbourne Maroochydore, Perth, Sydney, Brisbane, Gold Coast, Cairns, Townsville, Canberra, Sunshine Coast	B E H I M P S T **Graduate jobs** **Internships**	Page 138
#10	imc TRADING	**IMC Trading Australia** `4.5` ★★★★½ #2 in Trading	📍 Sydney	E I S **Graduate jobs** **Internships**	Page 138

L	Law, Legal Studies & Justice	
M	Medical & Health Sciences	
P	Property & Built Environment	
S	Sciences	
T	Teaching & Education	

Rank	Employer		Location of opportunities	Accepting applications from / Types of opportunities	Learn more
#11	KPMG	**KPMG Australia** 3.9 ★★★★☆ #3 in Accounting & advisory	Sydney, Melbourne, Canberra, Brisbane, Gold Coast, Perth, Adelaide, Darwin, Hobart, Parramatta, Wollongong, Geelong, Townsville	B C E H I L M P S T Graduate jobs Internships	Page 139
#12	FDM	**FDM Group Australia** 4.1 ★★★★☆ #2 in Technology	Sydney, Melbourne, Brisbane, Canberra	B C E H I L M P S T Graduate jobs	Page 139
#13	GHD	**GHD** 3.9 ★★★★☆ #2 in Engineering consulting	Australian Capital Territory, New South Wales, Northern Territory, Queensland, South Australia, Tasmania, Victoria, Western Australia	B C E H I L M P S T Graduate jobs Internships	Page 140
#14	L'ORÉAL	**L'Oréal Australia & New Zealand** 4.2 ★★★★☆ #1 in Retail & consumer goods	Melbourne, Auckland	B C E H I L M P S T Graduate jobs Internships	Page 140
#15	amazon	**Amazon** 4.2 ★★★★☆ #3 in Technology	Sydney, Melbourne, Brisbane, Adelaide, Canberra, Auckland, Wellington, Remote	B C E H I L M P S Graduate jobs Internships	Page 141
#16	WSP	**WSP Australia** 4.2 ★★★★☆ #3 in Engineering consulting	Australia wide	B C E H I L M P S Graduate jobs Internships	Page 141

Key for relevant degrees:

B Business & Management

C Creative Arts

E Engineering & Mathematics

H Humanities, Arts & Social Sciences

I IT & Computer Science

Rank	Employer	Location of opportunities	Accepting applications from / Types of opportunities	Learn more
#17	**BHP** 4.2 ★★★★☆ #1 in Mining, oil & gas	Queensland, South Australia, Western Australia	B E H I L M P S T Graduate jobs Internships	Page 142
#18	**ANZ** 4.4 ★★★★☆ #3 in Banking & financial servicess	Sydney, Melbourne, Perth, Adelaide, Brisbane	B C E H I L M P S T Graduate jobs Internships	Page 142
#19	**KEARNEY** 4.2 ★★★★☆ #3 in Management consulting	Sydney, Melbourne	B C E H I L M P S T Graduate jobs Internships	Page 143
#20	**Coles group** 4.2 ★★★★☆ #2 in Retail & consumer goods	Victoria	B C E H I L M P S T Graduate jobs	Page 143
#21	**Nous Group** 4.3 ★★★★☆ #4 in Management consulting	Melbourne, Sydney, Canberra, Brisbane, Perth, Darwin	B C E H I L M P S T Graduate jobs Internships	Page 144
#22	**BDO Australia** 4.2 ★★★★☆ #4 in Accounting & advisory	Perth, Sydney, Melbourne, Brisbane, Cairns, Adelaide, Hobart, Darwin	B C E H I L M P S Graduate jobs Internships	Page 144

L Law, Legal Studies & Justice	**M** Medical & Health Sciences	**P** Property & Built Environment	**S** Sciences	**T** Teaching & Education

Rank	Employer	Location of opportunities	Accepting applications from / Types of opportunities	Learn more
#23	**NSW Government** `3.9` ★★★★☆ #1 in Government & public service	⦿ Sydney	B C E H I L M P S T Graduate jobs Internships	Page 145
#24	**Mastercard Australia** `4.4` ★★★★½ #4 in Technology	⦿ Sydney, Melbourne	B C E H I L M P S T Graduate jobs Internships	Page 145
#25	**Quantium** `4.4` ★★★★½ #5 in Technology	⦿ Sydney, Melbourne, Canberra, work from home	B E I S Graduate jobs Internships	Page 146
#26	**Telstra** `4.0` ★★★★☆ #6 in Technology	⦿ Australia wide	B C E H I L M P S T Graduate jobs Internships	Page 146
#27	**Grant Thornton** `4.1` ★★★★☆ #5 in Accounting & advisory	⦿ Sydney, Melbourne, Brisbane, Adelaide, Cairns, Perth	B I L Graduate jobs Internships	Page 147
#28	**Jacobs Australia** `4.1` ★★★★☆ #4 in Engineering consulting	⦿ Sydney, Newcastle, Melbourne, Hobart, Adelaide, Perth, Darwin, Cairns, Townsville, Brisbane, Auckland, Christchurch, Wellington	B C E H I L M P S T Graduate jobs Internships	Page 147

Key for relevant degrees:

B Business & Management

C Creative Arts

E Engineering & Mathematics

H Humanities, Arts & Social Sciences

I IT & Computer Science

Rank	Employer	Location of opportunities	Accepting applications from / Types of opportunities	Learn more
#29	**Jarden** · 4.8 ★★★★★ · #4 in Banking & financial servicess	📍 Sydney, Melbourne	B E H I L M S · Graduate jobs · Internships	Page 148
#30	**RACV** · 4.3 ★★★★☆ · #5 in Banking & financial servicess	📍 Melbourne	B C E H I L M P S T · Graduate jobs	Page 148
#31	**Tibra Capital** · 4.1 ★★★★☆ · #3 in Trading	📍 Sydney, Wollongong, London	B E I S · Graduate jobs · Internships	Page 149
#32	**Accenture Australia and New Zealand** · 3.8 ★★★★☆ · #5 in Management consulting	📍 Sydney, Melbourne, Brisbane, Perth, Adelaide, Canberra, Auckland, Wellington	B C E H I L M P S T · Graduate jobs · Internships	Page 149
#33	**Department of Defence** · 4.1 ★★★★☆ · #2 in Government & public service	📍 Adelaide, Brisbane, Canberra, Cairns, Darwin, Melbourne, Newcastle, Perth, Sydney	B C E H I L M P S T · Graduate jobs · Internships	Page 150
#34	**BAE Systems Australia** · 3.9 ★★★★☆ · #1 in Defence & aerospace	📍 Sydney, Melbourne, Adelaide, Canberra, Newcastle, Perth	B E H I L M S T · Graduate jobs · Internships	Page 150

	L	Law, Legal Studies & Justice	M	Medical & Health Sciences	P	Property & Built Environment	S	Sciences	T	Teaching & Education

Rank	Employer		Location of opportunities	Accepting applications from / Types of opportunities	Learn more
#35	**Westpac Group** `4.4` ★★★★☆ #6 in Banking & financial servicess		⊙ New South Wales, Queensland, South Australia, Victoria, Western Australia	B C E H I L M P S T **Graduate jobs** Internships	Page 151
#36	**Schneider Electric Australia & New Zealand** `4.0` ★★★★☆ #7 in Technology		⊙ Sydney, Melbourne, Adelaide, Perth, Brisbane, Hobart, Auckland, Wellington, Christchurch	B C E H I L M P S T **Graduate jobs** Internships	Page 151
#37	**Optus** `3.9` ★★★★☆ #8 in Technology		⊙ Sydney	B C E H I L M P S T **Graduate jobs**	Page 152
#38	**Pitcher Partners** `4.2` ★★★★☆ #6 in Accounting & advisory		⊙ Melbourne	B E I L **Graduate jobs** Internships	Page 152
#39	**EY Australia** `3.8` ★★★★☆ #7 in Accounting & advisory		⊙ Australian Capital Territory, New South Wales, Northern Territory, Queensland, South Australia, Victoria, Western Australia	B C E H I L M P S T **Graduate jobs** Internships	Page 153
#40	**Herbert Smith Freehills** `4.4` ★★★★☆ #1 in Law		⊙ Brisbane, Melbourne, Perth, Sydney	L **Graduate jobs** Clerkships	Page 153

Key for relevant degrees:

B Business & Management	**C** Creative Arts	**E** Engineering & Mathematics
H Humanities, Arts & Social Sciences	**I** IT & Computer Science	

Rank	Employer	Location of opportunities	Accepting applications from / Types of opportunities	Learn more
#41	**Fuse Recruitment** — 4.3 ★★★★☆ — #1 in Recruitment & HR	Melbourne, Brisbane, Adelaide, Parramatta	B C E H I L M P S — Graduate jobs — Internships	Page 154
#42	**Australian Security Intelligence Organisation (ASIO)** — #3 in Government & public service	Canberra	B C E H I L M P S T — Graduate jobs	Page 154
#43	**Queensland Government** — 4.2 ★★★★☆ — #4 in Government & public service	Queensland	B C E H I L M P S T — Graduate jobs	Page 155
#44	**Rio Tinto** — 4.0 ★★★★☆ — #2 in Mining, oil & gas	Multiple locations in Australia and New Zealand	B E H I P S — Graduate jobs — Internships	Page 155
#45	**John Holland** — 4.3 ★★★★☆ — #1 in Construction & property services	Victoria, New South Wales, Queensland, Western Australia, Adelaide	B C E H I L M P S T — Graduate jobs — Internships	Page 156
#46	**Woodside Energy** — 3.9 ★★★★☆ — #3 in Mining, oil & gas	Perth, with some site based rotational opportunities available in Karratha	B C E H I L M P S T — Graduate jobs — Internships	Page 156

L Law, Legal Studies & Justice	**M** Medical & Health Sciences	**P** Property & Built Environment	**S** Sciences	**T** Teaching & Education

Rank	Employer		Location of opportunities	Accepting applications from / Types of opportunities	Learn more
#47	**Ashurst** `4.4` ★★★★⯪ #2 in Law		⊙ Sydney, Melbourne, Brisbane, Canberra, Perth	**L** Graduate jobs Clerkships	Page 157
#48	**Aurecon Australia** `4.1` ★★★★☆ #5 in Engineering consulting		⊙ Adelaide, Brisbane, Cairns, Canberra, Darwin, Gladstone, Gold Coast, Mackay, Maroochydore, Melbourne, Newcastle, Perth, Sydney, Toowoomb	**B C E H I L M P S T** Graduate jobs Internships	Page 157
#49	**Visagio** `4.6` ★★★★⯪ #6 in Management consulting		⊙ Australian Capital Territory, New South Wales, Northern Territory, Queensland, South Australia, Tasmania, Victoria, Western Australia	**B E I S** Graduate jobs Internships	Page 158
#50	**William Buck** `4.3` ★★★★☆ #8 in Accounting & advisory		⊙ Australia	**B L C** Graduate jobs Internships	Page 158
#51	**Susquehanna international Group (SIG)** `4.7` ★★★★★ #4 in Trading		⊙ Sydney	**B C E H I L M S** Graduate jobs Internships	Page 159
#52	**AECOM** `3.8` ★★★★☆ #6 in Engineering consulting		⊙ Adelaide, Brisbane, Cairns, Canberra, Darwin, Gold Coast, Newcastle, Mackay, Maroochydore, Melbourne, Perth, Rockhampton, Sydney, Townsville	**B E I P S** Graduate jobs Internships	Page 159

Key for relevant degrees:

B Business & Management	**C** Creative Arts	**E** Engineering & Mathematics
H Humanities, Arts & Social Sciences	**I** IT & Computer Science	

Rank	Employer		Location of opportunities	Accepting applications from / Types of opportunities	Learn more
#53	**Ramsay Health Care** 3.6 ★★★☆☆ #1 in Health		📍 Queensland, New South Wales, South Australia, Victoria, Western Australia	**M** Graduate jobs Internships	Page 160
#54	**AngloGold Ashanti Australia** 4.2 ★★★★☆ #4 in Mining, oil & gas		📍 Western Australia'	**B E H I M P S** Graduate jobs Internships	Page 160
#55	**Unilever Australia and New Zealand** 4.3 ★★★★☆ #3 in Retail & consumer goods		📍 Sydney, Auckland	**B C E H I L M P S T** Graduate jobs Internships	Page 161
#56	**Fujitsu** 4.6 ★★★★★ #9 in Technology		📍 Adelaide, Brisbane, Canberra, Melbourne, Sydney	**B C E H I L M P S T** Graduate jobs	Page 161
#57	**RSM Australia** 4.1 ★★★★☆ #9 in Accounting & advisory		📍 Multiple locations in Australia	**B E H I L M S** Graduate jobs Internships	Page 162
#58	**Shell** 4.8 ★★★★★ #5 in Mining, oil & gas		📍 Brisbane, Gladstone, Perth, Chinchilla	**B E I L M S** Graduate jobs Internships	Page 162

| | L | Law, Legal Studies & Justice | M | Medical & Health Sciences | P | Property & Built Environment | S | Sciences | T | Teaching & Education |

Rank	Employer		Location of opportunities	Accepting applications from / Types of opportunities	Learn more
#59	**Monadelphous** Monadelphous 4.1 ★★★★☆ **#2 in Construction & property services**		⊙ Brisbane, Perth	B E P S Graduate jobs Internships	Page 163
#60	Nova Systems **Nova Systems** 3.8 ★★★★☆ **#2 in Defence & aerospace**		⊙ Adelaide	B C E I M S Graduate jobs Internships	Page 163
#61	BOEING **Boeing Australia** 4.3 ★★★★☆ **#3 in Defence & aerospace**		⊙ Australian Capital Territory, New South Wales, Northern Territory, Queensland, South Australia, Victoria, Western Australia	B E I L S Graduate jobs Internships	Page 164
#62	Australian Government Australian Taxation Office **Australian Taxation Office (ATO)** 4.2 ★★★★☆ **#5 in Government & public service**		⊙ Adelaide, Albury, Brisbane, Canberra, Geelong, Gosford, Hobart, Melbourne, Newcastle, Perth, Sydney, Townsville, Wollongong	B C E H I L M P S T Graduate jobs	Page 164
#63	CSIRO **CSIRO** 4.4 ★★★★☆ **#1 in R&D and manufacturing**		⊙ Australian Capital Territory, New South Wales, Northern Territory, Queensland, South Australia, Tasmania, Victoria, Western Australia	B C E H I L M P S T Graduate jobs Internships	Page 165
#64	DXC TECHNOLOGY **DXC Technology** 3.3 ★★★☆☆ **#10 in Technology**		⊙ Australian Capital Territory, New South Wales, Northern Territory, Queensland, South Australia, Tasmania, Victoria, Western Australia	B C E H I L M P S T Graduate jobs	Page 165

Key for relevant degrees:

B Business & Management	**C** Creative Arts	**E** Engineering & Mathematics	**H** Humanities, Arts & Social Sciences	**I** IT & Computer Science

Rank	Employer	Location of opportunities	Accepting applications from / Types of opportunities	Learn more
#65	**Honeywell** 4.2 ★★★★☆ #11 in Technology	Australian Capital Territory, New South Wales, Queensland, Victoria, Western Australia, Auckland	B C E H I S — Graduate jobs — Internships	Page 166
#66	**SLB** 3.9 ★★★★☆ #12 in Technology	Queensland, South Australia, Western Australia, Global	E I S T — Graduate jobs — Internships	Page 166
#67	**Dulux Group** 4.3 ★★★★☆ #4 in Retail & consumer goods	New South Wales, Queensland, Victoria, South Australia, Western Australia	B C E H I L M P S T — Graduate jobs	Page 167
#68	**Protiviti** 3.6 ★★★☆☆ #7 in Management consulting	Brisbane, Canberra, Melbourne, Sydney	B C E H I L M P S T — Graduate jobs	Page 167
#69	**Stantec Australia** 4.1 ★★★★☆ #7 in Engineering consulting	Australia wide	B E I P S — Graduate jobs — Internships	Page 168
#70	**Kraft Heinz Company** 4.2 ★★★★☆ #5 in Retail & consumer goods	Melbourne, Seven Hills, Northgate	B C E H I L S — Graduate jobs	Page 168

| | | L | Law, Legal Studies & Justice | M | Medical & Health Sciences | P | Property & Built Environment | S | Sciences | T | Teaching & Education |

Rank	Employer	Location of opportunities	Accepting applications from / Types of opportunities	Learn more
#71	**SW Accountants & Advisors** **4.3** ★★★★☆ #10 in Accounting & advisory	⊙ Sydney, Brisbane, Melbourne, Perth	B E I L S **Graduate jobs** Internships	Page 169
#72	**TAL Australia** **4.4** ★★★★½ #7 in Banking & financial servicess	⊙ Sydney	B E H I L M S **Graduate jobs** Internships	Page 169
#73	**VivCourt Trading** **4.7** ★★★★★ #5 in Trading	⊙ Sydney, work from home	E I S **Graduate jobs** Internships	Page 170
#74	**Akuna Capital** **4.4** ★★★★☆ #6 in Trading	⊙ Sydney	B E I S T **Graduate jobs** Internships	Page 170
#75	**Allens** **4.5** ★★★★½ #3 in Law	⊙ Sydney, Melbourne, Brisbane, Perth	L **Graduate jobs** Clerkships	Page 171
#76	**Transgrid** **4.3** ★★★★☆ #1 in Energy & utilities	⊙ New South Wales	B C E H I L M P S T **Graduate jobs** Internships	Page 171

Key for relevant degrees:

B Business & Management

C Creative Arts

E Engineering & Mathematics

H Humanities, Arts & Social Sciences

I IT & Computer Science

Rank	Employer	Location of opportunities	Accepting applications from / Types of opportunities	Learn more
#77	**Dolby Australia** `4.5` ★★★★☆ #13 in Technology	⦿ Sydney	C E I · Graduate jobs · Internships	Page 172
#78	**McGrathNicol** `4.2` ★★★★☆ #11 in Accounting & advisory	⦿ Brisbane, Canberra, Melbourne, Perth, Sydney	B C E H I L S · Graduate jobs · Internships	Page 172
#79	**Department of the Prime Minister and Cabinet (PM&C)** `4.2` ★★★★☆ #6 in Government & public service	⦿ Canberra	B C E H I L M P S T · Graduate jobs · Internships	Page 173
#80	**Australian Energy Market Operator (AEMO)** `4.4` ★★★★☆ #2 in Energy & utilities	⦿ Melbourne, Sydney, Norwest, Brisbane, Perth, Adelaide	B E I S · Graduate jobs · Internships	Page 173
#81	**Bank of Queensland (BOQ)** `4.2` ★★★★☆ #8 in Banking & financial servicess	⦿ Brisbane, Sydney, Melbourne	B C E H I L M P S · Graduate jobs · Internships	Page 174
#82	**Mineral Resources** `4.3` ★★★★☆ #6 in Mining, oil & gas	⦿ Western Australia	B C E H I L M P S · Graduate jobs · Internships	Page 174

L Law, Legal Studies & Justice	**M** Medical & Health Sciences	**P** Property & Built Environment	**S** Sciences	**T** Teaching & Education

Rank	Employer	Location of opportunities	Accepting applications from / Types of opportunities	Learn more
#83	**Lockheed Martin** **4.0** ★★★★☆ #4 in Defence & aerospace	◉ Adelaide, Canberra	B E H I S L T Graduate jobs Internships	Page 175
#84	**ACCIONA Australia and New Zealand** **4.2** ★★★★☆ #3 in Construction & property services	◉ Queensland, New South Wales, Victoria, South Australia, Western Australia, New Zealand	B C E H I L M P S Graduate jobs	Page 175
#85	**Safe Work Australia** **4.4** ★★★★☆ #7 in Government & public service	◉ Canberra	B C E H I L M P S Graduate jobs	Page 176
#86	**Department of Energy, Environment and Climate Action (DEECA)** **4.2** ★★★★☆ #8 in Government & public service	◉ Melbourne, regional Victoria	B E H I M P S Graduate jobs	Page 176
#87	**Northrop Consulting Engineers** **4.5** ★★★★½ #8 in Engineering consulting	◉ Victoria, New South Wales, Queensland	E P T Graduate jobs Internships	Page 177
#88	**Xero Australia** **4.1** ★★★★☆ #14 in Technology	◉ Melbourne, Canberra	B C E H I L M P S T Graduate jobs Internships	Page 177

Key for relevant degrees:

B Business & Management	**C** Creative Arts	**E** Engineering & Mathematics
H Humanities, Arts & Social Sciences	**I** IT & Computer Science	

Rank	Employer	Location of opportunities	Accepting applications from / Types of opportunities	Learn more
#89	**Leidos Australia** ▲ leidos `4.1` ★★★★☆ #5 in Defence & aerospace	📍 Melbourne, Canberra	B C E H I L S T **Graduate jobs** **Internships**	Page 178
#90	**Tata Consultancy Services Australia and New Zealand** TATA CONSULTANCY SERVICES `4.2` ★★★★☆ #8 in Management consulting	📍 New South Wales, Victoria, New Zealand	B E I **Graduate jobs** **Internships**	Page 178
#91	**South32** SOUTH32 `4.2` ★★★★☆ #7 in Mining, oil & gas	📍 New South Wales, Queensland, Western Australia, Northern Territory	B E I M S **Graduate jobs** **Internships**	Page 179
#92	**Department of Health and Aged Care** Australian Government Department of Health and Aged Care `4.2` ★★★★☆ #9 in Government & public service	📍 Canberra	B C E H I L M P S T **Graduate jobs**	Page 179
#93	**nbn** nbn `4.2` ★★★★☆ #15 in Technology	📍 Sydney, Melbourne	B C E H I L M P S T **Graduate jobs**	Page 180
#94	**Rheinmetall** `4.4` ★★★★½ #6 in Defence & aerospace	📍 Brisbane, Melbourne, Adelaide	B E I **Graduate jobs** **Internships**	Page 180

L Law, Legal Studies & Justice	**M** Medical & Health Sciences	**P** Property & Built Environment	**S** Sciences	**T** Teaching & Education

Rank	Employer		Location of opportunities	Accepting applications from / Types of opportunities	Learn more
#95	Victorian Government	**3.8** ★★★★☆ #10 Government & public service	⊙ Melbourne	B C E H I L M P S T Graduate jobs	Page 181
#96	Clayton Utz	**3.8** ★★★★☆ #4 in Law	⊙ Sydney, Melbourne, Brisbane, Perth, Canberra	L Graduate jobs Clerkships	Page 181
#97	GSK	**4.5** ★★★★★ #1 in Pharmaceuticals	⊙ Melbourne, Sydney, Auckland	B C E H I L M P S T Graduate jobs Internships	Page 182
#98	CSL	**4.2** ★★★★☆ #2 in Pharmaceuticals	⊙ Melbourne	B E M S Graduate jobs Internships	Page 182
#99	MinterEllison	**4.3** ★★★★☆ #5 in Law	⊙ Sydney, Melbourne, Canberra, Darwin, Perth, Brisbane, Adelaide, work from home	B C E H I L M P S T Graduate jobs Clerkships	Page 183
#100	FTI Consulting	**4.2** ★★★★☆ #12 in Accounting & advisory	⊙ Sydney, Brisbane, Melbourne, Perth	B E H I L P S T Graduate jobs Internships	Page 183

Where curiosity **meets purpose.**

How you'll make a difference

At the Department of the Prime Minister and Cabinet (PM&C), our mission is to improve the lives of all Australians through high quality advice and support to the Government.

PM&C's Graduate Program provides an exciting, hands-on experience supporting the Prime Minister, Cabinet, Portfolio Ministers and Assistant Ministers. No matter your background, you'll bring your expertise to a range of projects and policies across the department. With opportunities for growth and development, this program is the perfect platform to jumpstart your career and make a difference.

We offer a unique graduate program where you will gain practical experience and diverse opportunities tailored to you.

For more, visit *pmc.gov.au/graduates*

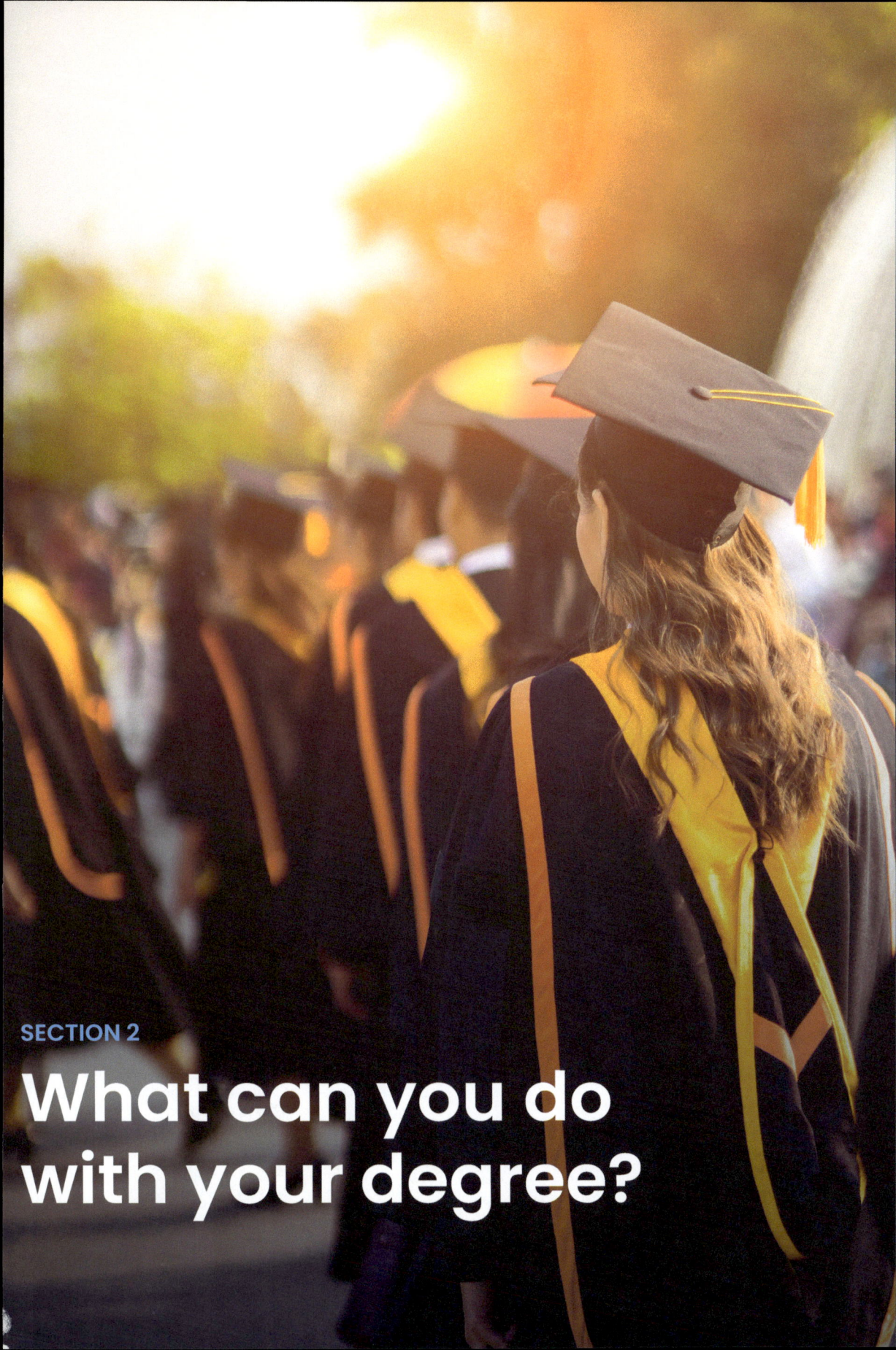

SECTION 2

What can you do with your degree?

What can you do with your degree?

If you've checked the Top 100 Employers list, you may have been surprised to find that employers are hiring students with all sorts of degrees!

This is because – outside of a handful of highly-regulated fields like accounting, medicine, and law – employers aren't too fussy about what you study. In fact, top employers (think: Apple, EY, General Motors, and JP Morgan) have been relaxing degree requirements all around the world.

At the end of the day, employers just want to know you can do the job – and that has more to do with your skill set than the letters on your diploma.

So what does your degree mean to employers, given this context?

Accounting

Even if you don't plan on working in the field, your accounting degree signals the following qualities to employers.

Financial expertise: You know how to think about a business' finances and understand what numbers matter most to the bottom line.

Attention to detail: If you've done well in your accounting courses, you probably have a good eye for detail – a skill that a surprising number of people don't have.

Work ethic & time management skills: Accounting programs are known for being demanding, requiring students to be organised, manage their time effectively, and meet deadlines consistently.

What do accounting grads actually do in the real world? Besides accounting, we've seen them working in areas as diverse as consulting, trading, policy, HR, and more. Find out more in our article.

Scan to read the full article on what you can do with your **accounting** degree

Business, management & commerce

To employers, a degree in business, management or commerce shows you might have the following skills.

Commercial awareness: You're familiar with how businesses operate and thrive, and have a broad understanding of how each part of an organisation – from logistics to HR to marketing – contributes to its success.

Analytical skills: Understanding data, market trends, and financial reports is key in business. With these skills, you're able to piece together clues to solve complex business problems.

Management skills: These programs often teach you how to motivate teams and manage projects effectively, both important skills in the workplace.

Typically, grads with this background land jobs in consulting, banking and finance. But we've also seen some going into tech, government, and other fields. For more ideas, check out our article on this topic.

Scan to read the full article on what you can do with your **business, management & commerce** degree

Arts

To employers, a Bachelor of Arts (BA) degree hints that you may have some of the following skills.

Communication skills: Whether it's through writing, speaking, or even expressing ideas through media, arts graduates know how to convey their thoughts clearly and persuasively.

Cultural awareness: Studying arts often involves exploring diverse cultures, histories, and philosophies. This can make you a pro at understanding different perspectives and building relationships in a globalised workplace.

Creative thinking skills: Arts courses push you to think outside the box and be original with your ideas. Employers in industries from tech to marketing are on the lookout for people who can think differently and spark innovation.

This doesn't mean you're limited to non-technical fields though. These days, there are BA grads who learn to code and land jobs in software development! For more ideas on what arts students do in the real world, check out our article on this topic.

Scan to read the full article on what you can do with your **arts** degree

Law

Many employers will look at a law degree and assume you have some of the following skills and qualities.

Legal awareness: Lots of careers across a diverse range of industries benefit from people who are familiar with the law and know how to apply legal principles.

Research & analytical skills: Legal education emphasises meticulous research, making law students adept at finding and analysing information.

Communication skills: Whether it's drafting a contract, arguing a case, or simply negotiating terms, law graduates are masters of written and verbal communication and great at presenting information logically and convincingly.

Unsurprisingly, law firms aren't the only employers who'll look favourably on your degree. Our surveys have uncovered law grads working in corporate tax, management consulting, risk management, policy, investigative work, and more.

Scan to read the full article on what you can do with your **law** degree

Healthcare

A degree in healthcare tells employers that you possess a unique blend of technical and interpersonal skills.

Attention to detail: Precision is paramount in healthcare, which means you likely have a better eye for detail than most of your peers.

Teamwork: Healthcare is inherently collaborative. Your degree has likely involved working in multidisciplinary teams, preparing you to be an effective team player.

Integrity & a strong work ethic: Students in the health & medical sciences tend to have a good moral compass paired with a strong work ethic.

Our data has found healthcare grads working in fields like government & public service, mining, oil & gas, management consulting, and more.

Scan to read the full article on what you can do with your **healthcare** degree

IT & computer science

What does an IT or computer science degree tell employers about you? Likely that you have some of the following skills and attributes.

Tech savvy: Your education not only equips you with a foundation in current technologies but also prepares you to learn and adapt quickly to new tools and languages as they emerge.

Analytical thinking: You're probably able to approach data and systems analytically, making reasoned decisions based on evidence.

Problem-solving skills: Like engineering students, you're likely good at breaking down complex issues, identifying root causes, and designing solutions – skills that are highly sought after across industries.

These days, basically every sector is in need of tech talent, so you won't have issues finding a job in a sector of your choice. And if you prefer to do non-IT work, we've also seen grads with your background working in banking, finance, management consulting, and more.

Scan to read the full article on what you can do with your **IT & computer** degree

Science

A degree in the sciences opens up doors to careers in many fields. That's because to employers, your degree indicates that you have a solid foundation in several key areas.

Analytical thinking: You're trained to analyse data and draw logical conclusions, essential for roles that demand precision and critical thinking.

Quantitative skills: Your ability to think through problems with math is applicable in industries from tech to finance.

Attention to detail: Your ability to focus on minute details ensures accuracy, a trait highly valued in many professional settings.

We've seen science grads land roles in everything from tech and finance to government and consulting.

Scan to read the full article on what you can do with your **science** degree

Education

A degree in education signals to employers that you are equipped with qualities and capabilities like the ones that follow.

Excellent communication skills: Your degree likely trained you to convey complex ideas in clear, understandable ways, crucial for any role that involves instruction, presentation, or team communication.

Leadership skills: With training in classroom management and instructional leadership, you're prepared to guide others, whether students or colleagues, towards achieving their goals. This skill is invaluable in managerial or supervisory positions.

Patience & empathy: Educators are trained to be patient and empathetic, essential for fostering a supportive and effective learning or working environment.

A degree in education prepares you not just for traditional teaching roles but also for positions that require strong interpersonal skills. Our surveys have found education grads going into fields like marketing, management consulting, human resources, and more.

Scan to read the full article on what you can do with your **education** degree

Engineering

Employers tend to assume engineering students have the following skills and traits.

Problem-solving skills: Engineering education is centred around solving complex problems. You're likely good at breaking large issues down into manageable parts, analysing these components, and devising efficient solutions.

'Can-do' attitude: Equipped with strong problem-solving abilities, you probably also feel ready to tackle new and unfamiliar challenges, turning potential obstacles into opportunities for growth – something employers like to see.

Quantitative analysis: Engineering students are comfortable using maths and scientific principles, a skill valued in many fields.

It's no surprise that many engineers work in mining, construction, and manufacturing. Our surveys have also uncovered engineering grads working in fields as diverse as finance to patent examination to technical sales.

Scan to read the full article on what you can do with your **engineering** degree

So what can you do with your degree?

The answer is 'Anything if you put your mind to it!' This might sound cliche, but it's true. Employers will look at your degree and assume a thing or two about what skills you have (and don't have). But it won't be the only thing they look at!

So if your degree doesn't cover all the skills you need for a dream job, beef up your CV with internships, volunteer work, student organisations, coursework, and any other experiences or achievements that'll help you make your case.

Luckily, employers are a lot more open-minded about degrees these days – which is why you'll see science grads in finance and arts students in tech.

Don't believe us? Then read the following real stories from grads who've taken some interesting turns in their career.

On the job

DeClan McGann

Bachelor of Commerce and Global Studies (Marketing Science/German Studies); Monash University

Graduate Analyst at RACV

RACV

'In many ways, my diverse qualifications and experiences have been a blessing rather than a curse, as employers in the space are always looking for broad perspectives and experiences.'

What's your job about?

Best known for its Roadside Assistance service and Motor Insurance products – RACV offers a diverse range of products and services including insurance, on-call assistance, loans, resorts, and solar installation among many others. As a data analyst, my day-to-day activities are incredibly varied and dependent on what has been deemed a priority. When assigned a project or task, there are generally three stages that we go through: Building logic, analysis and visualisation, then presentation and review.

What's your background?

I went to Monash to complete a double degree in Commerce and Global Studies. I had an interest in Marketing and Business but also wanted to further my German language studies. This led to me spending half a year abroad at the European Business School in Frankfurt, which was a unique opportunity to further my business studies while also strengthening my German.

After graduating in 2020, I took a job as a Sales Consultant for a Truck bodybuilder. Doing this during the pandemic was exceptionally difficult as visiting potential customers was almost impossible. I was considering going back to Uni to complete a Masters in Business Analytics at Melbourne, before being offered a grad role in the Analytics team at RACV in October 2021.

Could someone with a different background do your job?

As someone with a background that was very much outside the Data Analytics space (aside from some basic coding that I had learnt online in my spare time), I would encourage anyone with an interest in the field to give it a try. In many ways, my diverse qualifications and experiences have been a blessing rather than a curse, as employers in the space are always looking for broad perspectives and experiences. To succeed in the space, employers are looking for good problem-solving skills, as well as an appetite to continuously learn and develop.

What's the coolest thing about your job?

It satisfies my inner curiosity, allowing me to go down the proverbial rabbit hole in search of a finding or an insight that may have a significant impact on how business is done. I have never felt satisfied in a job where the impact my work was having was either invisible or non-existent and despite being relatively inexperienced and new to the field, I can see the impact that my work and effort are making.

What are the limitations of your job?

As the majority of the work isn't day-to-day, we are very rarely dealing with cookie-cutter problems and as a result, very rarely create cookie-cutter solutions. This means that one has to be constantly thinking outside the box, as well as finding and fixing bugs or problems with the code or visualisations that we are creating.

Scan to read more **graduate stories**

On the job

Katie Wylie

Bachelor of Criminology
and Criminal Justice

Adviser at Department
of the Prime Minister and
Cabinet (PM&C)

'This job is about so much more than what you know about Government or politics. It's the skills and experience you have from past jobs and completing a university degree, it's the passion you have for the areas that you care about, and it's becoming immersed in work or conversations and realising you have a genuine curiosity to learn more.'

Scan to
read more
graduate stories

My experience as someone who wasn't very aware of politics and Government in General.

When I first started applying for graduate programs in Canberra, I was concerned that I wouldn't know enough about Government or politics to either get the role, or to be able to perform well in it. I had never paid much attention to local or federal Government, and coming from a background in social sciences, I didn't have the same exposure that my Political Science or International Relations friends did.

As I started to apply for jobs, I made sure to figure out what areas I was interested in and had a genuine passion for. I paid attention to the areas of focus and recent work that different Departments had completed to narrow down where I would apply, and found that this research also helped during the application process (especially when completing writing tasks).

When I started at Prime Minister and Cabinet (PM&C), I realised that people in the Department had a wide range of knowledge regarding Government processes and politics in general. I found it reassuring that not everyone was an expert, and you are still able to complete high-quality work and participate in work conversations without feeling left behind.

As we went through the year, both the Entry Level Programs team and the rotations that I went through were really invested in my learning and development. As a Grad, you're given a lot of opportunities to attend training sessions, and this really fast-tracks your learning. I've started to listen, read and watch more content related to Government and now that I'm dealing with these topics on a daily basis, it's easier to understand and be invested in what's going on.

While there is an advantage to people who have completed relevant degrees or who keep up to date with Government, this job is about so much more than what you know about Government or politics. It's the skills and experience you have from past jobs and completing a university degree, it's the passion you have for the areas that you care about, and it's becoming immersed in work or conversations and realising you have a genuine curiosity to learn more.

I'm really glad that I did apply to these programs – I've used elements of my degree and past work experience to succeed within the program, and I've gotten some amazing experiences already (contributing to a speech the PM gave, working on the COVID-19 Health Response, and writing briefs for the Secretary). I would highly recommend anyone from any degree and with any amount of previous work experience to apply – your value adds to the Department isn't what you know, but what you can do.

On the job

Amelia Rogers

Bachelor of Arts and Law;
Australian Catholic University

Graduate in Employee
Relations at NSW Government

NSW GOVERNMENT

'While Employee
Relations does have
a legal element
to it, there is no
requirement of a law
degree – if you're
an excellent planner
and communicator,
you will thrive in
this area.'

How did you choose your specialisation?

To be honest, I had never really considered Employee Relations! While I had an idea of where I would like to go professionally, I didn't want to limit myself to specific career options and wanted to challenge myself with new experiences, which is why I was drawn to the NSW Government Graduate Program. I found this in Employee Relations and working in this area made me develop a new passion for an area of law I hadn't previously considered exploring. Prior to this, I was considering specialising in either criminal law or consumer law.

What does your employer do?

The Department of Communities and Justice is the amalgamation of the Department of Family and Community Services and the Department of Justice. It supports our society's most vulnerable people and families to participate in social and economic life while providing legal, court and supervision services to the people of NSW in order to create stronger communities.

What are your areas of responsibility?

Employee Relations manages the relationship between the Department and its employees through union liaison and other relevant judicial bodies and provides advice to the Department on employment law. I help coordinate meetings and consultations with the unions and assist on industrial relations and employment law matters at the Industrial Relations Commission, NSW Civil and Administrative Tribunal (NCAT), and other tribunals.

What are the career prospects with your job?

Almost every business, both public and private, has an industrial relations element and needs someone to facilitate an effective relationship between the employees and the employer, as well as someone to provide advice on employment law. You can find private-sector equivalents almost everywhere, and internal growth is excellent from both a legal and non-legal aspect. This area is a great combination of administrative and employment law and human resources.

Could someone with a different background do your job?

Absolutely! While Employee Relations does have a legal element to it, there is no requirement of a law degree – if you're an excellent planner and communicator, you will thrive in this area.

What's the biggest limitation of your job?

The work in Employee Relations is quite reactive, so there are times when the workload can increase substantially with little warning. Sometimes it can get quite stressful, but I found that the best way to avoid stress is to stay focused and prepare everything as early as I can so I can adapt to any sudden surprises along the way. The team is also always happy to help if I need it, which is a great comfort. I have never had to work on weekends.

Scan to
read more
graduate stories

au.prosple.com

On the job

Victoria Xu

Bachelor of Global Studies, Master of Human Resource Management; Monash University, University of Melbourne

People & Culture Graduate at Coles

coles group

'Coles is very supportive in providing opportunities for team members to move laterally so that they can broaden their knowledge and skills in different areas of the business.'

What support is given to you?

One of the best things about the graduate program is the extensive support network you will receive. When you do commence the graduate program, you are assigned a buddy who is either a previous or current graduate in your function. Your function will also partner you with an accelerator coach who is a senior leader within the business and will assist you with navigating your career journey at Coles. During my time rotating in different teams, I've been paired up with someone in the team who becomes your day-to-day mentor. Additionally, you will receive support from your line manager, the broader team as well as the leadership team. There are always opportunities and events to connect with other team members and leaders within the business.

What do you enjoy most about your role?

What I love the most about my role in People & Culture is the fact that I service the business. I have always enjoyed connecting and learning about people, and through this role, it has been interesting to be able to support business decisions and projects through a 'people' lens. I am always putting team members at the forefront in every facet of my work, so it has been extremely rewarding to see the impact that I make at an individual level.

Why Coles?

I chose to apply for Coles because of how many opportunities there are to develop your career. Within People & Culture, there are so many teams that specialise in different areas of HR which you won't necessarily get in many other organisations. Coles is very supportive in providing opportunities for team members to move laterally so that they can broaden their knowledge and skills in different areas of the business. During my graduate program, I have completed rotations that cross over with the Digital and Supply Chain functions and am now completing a rotation in the Legal and safety team.

What is the coolest experience you've had in this function so far?

One of the coolest experiences I've had so far would have to be being involved in the launch of the Redbank Automated Distribution Centre in Queensland, one of the largest automated grocery warehouses in Australia. I was heavily involved in creating, designing, and putting together the recruitment process for the site. To not only see the work you've done come to life in person but also see the candidates that you interviewed to commence their role at the site was really special. It's also really cool to be on a project that receives so much media attention, and even have the Prime Minister visit the site for the launch.

Scan to read more **graduate stories**

On the job

Hunter Conochie

Bachelor of Engineering
(Mechatronic Engineering);
University of Queensland

Graduate Software Engineer
at Rheinmetall

'You do not have to have studied software engineering. Many of the best software engineers I know actually studied physics or geology and then moved across for better pay and work/life balance.'

What's your job about?

One of the contracts with the Commonwealth of Australia supported by Rheinmetall Defence Australia (RDA) is the Land-400 project which is supplying new Combat Reconnaissance Vehicles to the Australian Army. I am responsible for helping my team develop a general vehicle architecture for this new era of vehicles. My current project at RDA is interfacing with the software development team and the systems engineers to work out how we can test and evaluate the software to ensure it is robust and acceptable, given the accepted requirements specified by the Commonwealth of Australia.

What's your background?

I always knew I wanted to study engineering but what type of engineering was the hard bit. So, I chose mechatronics to get a bit of everything. I never really liked software at University but once I got a bit better at it and realised I could work from home or anywhere with just a laptop, I was drawn to the profession. The best semester I had was my semester abroad in Sweden to study. I visited 25 countries and met plenty of amazing people that I still talk to, from all over the world.

Could someone with a different background do your job?

Yes, many people come from different backgrounds in software. You DO NOT have to have studied software engineering. Many of the best software engineers I know actually studied physics or geology and then moved across for better pay and work/life balance. Must be willing to learn constantly. Software is a huge world, you'll never learn it all. Being good at asking for help from the more experienced guys, can save you a lot of time.

What's the coolest thing about your job?

I love the software at Rheinmetall because of the flexibility to learn and also get my code on the final product. There is a great mix of responsibility but also flexibility. You can set your own pace being a graduate at Rheinmetall. RDA is happy for you to just learn and take things in and partner with more senior engineers if that is what you want to do.

3 pieces of advice for yourself when you were a student...

- Take better notes of things you might need in the future, and collate it all.

- Study the theory, not the practice. e.g. A subject on algorithms will be more important than solar panels as its more useful across a wider domain of industry and jobs.

- Try to make studying more enjoyable by investing in your learning. Buy nice stationary, go to a café, reward yourself after 2 hours etc.

Scan to
read more
graduate stories

On the job

Sarah Aldrich

Bachelor of Science (Biology);
University of Sydney

Graduate Policy Officer at
NSW Government

NSW GOVERNMENT

'I love that my job allows me to make a difference in the lives of the people of NSW and the environment in NSW.'

How did you get to your current job position?

I started off studying a Bachelor of Veterinary Biology/Doctor of Veterinary Medicine at the University of Sydney but after two years decided this wasn't for me and transferred to a Bachelor of Science majoring in Biology. After I decided to become a veterinarian wasn't for me I started to brainstorm what kind of career I might like to pursue. I was immediately attracted to jobs in the public sector and discovered the NSW Government Graduate Program and applied. I started in the Program at the Department of Planning, Industry and Environment (DPIE.)

What does your employer do?

My team at DPIE is working on developing the Cumberland Plain Conservation Plan (CPCP) for the bio-certification of growth areas in Western Sydney. This involves strategically planning the location and management of conservation sites which offset the damage caused by development in growth areas.

What are your areas of responsibility?

My main responsibilities include helping create, edit and update the Monitoring, Evaluation and Reporting framework for the CPCP, and helping manage the team's relationships with our stakeholders and delivery partners. I acted as the single point of contact between the branch and a consultancy firm and acted as secretariat at a weekly meeting with them. I conducted a lot of research projects when I was in the branch from researching the potential use of blockchain technology for our project to researching possible survey methods for the different threatened species in our project area.

What are the career prospects with your job?

The Graduate Program offers a stepping stone to a career in the public sector. After we successfully complete the Program, we are offered a permanent role in our home agency (mine being DPIE). The Graduate Program allows the grounding to apply for jobs in different agencies and in the private sector. The skills I have learnt so far in the Program will be applicable to many different roles.

What do you love the most about your job?

I love that my job allows me to make a difference in the lives of the people of NSW and the environment in NSW. I love that my job allows me to have a good work-life balance, mentoring, networking, training and skill development. I also love that I am exposed to a wide variety of different tasks and my managers have both really tried to help me develop my skills in my areas of interest.

What's the biggest limitation of your job?

Having three six-month rotations is good for access to a variety of tasks and workplaces – it can feel a little difficult moving as you feel as though you are just getting the hang of everything before you are moved to another place, but this does not detract from the Program. In the way of stress, I bear a level of responsibility suitable for me and if I ever need help with anything, I am always able to get support from my team.

On the job

Alanah Hall

Bachelor of Applied Science (Physiotherapy); University of Sydney

Claims Consultant at TAL Australia

TAL

'My medical knowledge and background helped me transition from a Physio to a Claims Consultant... Having an allied health background has helped me understand the treatment and potentially some extra services we can provide to assist our customers in their recovery'

What's your background?

I studied a Bachelor of Applied Science (Physiotherapy) and worked for a number of private clinics for a few years before moving into the Life Insurance industry. I started off as a Claims Consultant before moving into a Rehab Consultant role. I then transitioned from Westpac to TAL, moving back into the Claims team as a Claims Consultant once again.

Tell us a little bit about working in Claims at TAL (what it involves, how you learn, what new skills and knowledge have you developed in this time)?

We spend each and every day assisting customers throughout what is usually a very difficult time in their lives. It involves a very high level of empathy – we really need to put ourselves in their shoes to understand just how life-changing their illness could be, how it affects their everyday lives and what we can do to make it easier on them. You learn to be a very good listener and communicator. It has definitely made me a kinder person – you start to understand just how important life insurance is for people in their time of need and how providing a high level of service can really brighten their day.

What were some transferable skills that you have brought to TAL from your previous career?

My medical knowledge and background helped me transition from a Physio to a Claims Consultant. Additionally, my ability to understand function translates into everyday tasks and how a lack of function can prevent someone from returning to work. Having an allied health background has helped me understand the treatment and potentially some extra services we can provide to assist our customers in their recovery. Above all, working in healthcare provided me time to perfect my communication skills, which is the single most important skill we need in claims.

Tell us about some of the things that attracted you to this line of work?

The work-life balance! TAL is extremely flexible, allowing us to work from home three days per week. This cuts down travel time and means we have more time left in the day to spend with the ones we love the most. There are a number of perks, including lifestyle days, ongoing learning opportunities and an amazing office culture!

3 pieces of advice to anyone thinking about making a career change into Claims or the Life Insurance Industry:

- People choose to work in healthcare because they have a desire to help people. Although this is in a different way, we spend every minute of the day helping those in need.

- Really embrace the culture – this is a great place to work, and we spend so much time with our colleagues – make the most of it and get to know people through attending social events and making friends

- Ask questions! There is so much support and so many people here to help you through your transition, you will never feel alone.

Scan to read more **graduate stories**

On the job

Eromanga Adermann

Bachelor of Science
(Mathematics and Physics),
Doctor of Philosphy - PhD,
Physics (Cosmology
and Astrophysics);
University of Sydney

Insights & Data Consultant
- Artificial Intelligence
Engineering at CSIRO

**'I studied to become
a research scientist,
which, perhaps
unsurprisingly,
requires skills that
are great to have in
consulting.'**

How have your studies helped you in your current role at Capgemini?

I have a Bachelor of Science (Advanced Mathematics) and a PhD in Cosmology and Astrophysics from the University of Sydney. I studied to become a research scientist, which, perhaps unsurprisingly, requires skills that are great to have in consulting. My science degrees helped me develop critical thinking and analytical skills, which are needed to deconstruct and reframe problems in consulting, as well as creative thinking skills, which are required to produce innovative solutions to hard problems. I also learned to code during my studies, which has opened the door to the AI space for me.

What are you passionate about in your role?

I love the process of solving problems. There is a nice feeling of satisfaction that comes with finishing a project or a challenging task! I also love helping people in some way, and if what I did has made things easier or in other ways benefited them, then it makes me happy. I also love exploring the possibilities for how technology will evolve and imagining what the future could be like, and in my role, I get to be in the thick of cutting-edge technology.

What does a typical day look like for you and what are you currently working on?

There isn't really a typical day for me, which is typical for consulting! I partake in a variety of different activities, both for clients and Capgemini. I am currently analysing business data to help remediate a data security issue at a client and automating several business processes that would be extremely tedious to do manually. Beyond that, I'm also working with the Social Innovators group to help Capgemini make a positive impact, and helping out with initiatives like Women at Capgemini.

How would you describe the culture at Capgemini?

I love the culture here at Capgemini! It's a wonderful mix of team spirit, fun and freedom. We work hard, but we make it enjoyable. One of the most amazing things about Capgemini is that everyone is so friendly and supportive. If there's anything you're not happy about, there are people around you who are willing to help. There is also a lot of freedom to build your career here at Capgemini. If you want to try out different types of work or move into a different capability, there are people who will help you do that.

What have you gained from working at Capgemini from a career perspective?

I have gained a far better understanding of the technology landscape and what the world could look like in the near future. I've also been able to develop skills in areas of interest to me, specifically in automation, data science, and AI. Non-career wise: The most valuable thing I have gained from working at Capgemini is life-long friendships.

Scan to
read more
graduate stories

On the job

Amelia McGrath

Bachelor of Business and Arts;
Monash University

Management Trainee
at L'Oréal Australia and
New Zealand

L'ORÉAL

'I love seeing campaigns come to life – through the creative process, filming on set or through new product presentations. The way that our team works together is electric and there's always an opportunity to learn something new.'

What's your job about?

Our brand team works to keep us on top by creating exciting activations in-store, launching the hottest products, rethinking how we can amplify the user experience, and engaging with consumers and retailers to build connections with our stakeholders.

As a Maybelline brand marketing grad, you could be briefing and workshopping new campaigns with agencies or working with retailers to decide which stock you'll see on our displays. You might be working with suppliers to create new packaging for our products or attending shoots for our advertisements and voiceovers.

One of the most exciting things I've worked on has been presenting new launches to our management committee, and deciding which products and shades will be perfect for our market. I've also recently been working through sourcing optimisation projects to prevent supply chain disruptions, allowing us to get makeup into the hands of our customers. And with all the fun, there are also the more logistical, day-to-day tasks that you complete.

What's your background?

A different journey to most, I was an elite gymnast until I was 18. I worked hard enough to represent Australia internationally and compete in Olympic Trials. School took a backseat for most of this journey so when I left gymnastics, I really had no idea who I was or what I wanted to be. I started a short-lived psychology degree... turns out science wasn't for me! At 19, I enrolled in an after-hours Diploma of Makeup whilst working full time, ultimately landing a retail artist job at MAC. I loved making people feel good about themselves but wanted to be on the other side of the industry – designing campaigns, launching products and shaping the way people experienced cosmetics. So, I made the (daunting) decision to go back to uni at 22 and study for a Bachelor of Business and Arts.

In my final year of uni, I received an offer for L'Oreal's Marketing Management Trainee Program – my dream offer!

Could someone with a different background do your job?

Anyone can do this role, but I think there are a few key skills that you need to thrive. Most importantly, being able to think on your feet and take challenges head-on. A good dose of optimism and resilience is key. Loving beauty helps, too!

What's the coolest thing about your job?

I love seeing campaigns come to life – through the creative process, filming on set or through new product presentations. The way that our team works together is electric and there's always an opportunity to learn something new. I love learning and trying new things and Maybelline is the perfect launchpad to dive in headfirst and make an impact.

Scan to
read more
graduate stories

What sectors can you work in?

Accounting & advisory 40

Banking, trading & financial services 46

Construction & property services 52

Defence, R&D & manufacturing 58

Engineering consulting 64

Government & public service 70

Law 76

Management consulting 82

Mining, energy, oil & gas 88

Retail & consumer goods 94

Technology 100

Accounting & advisory

Advisory

Advisory services are like a doctor offering tips on how to get healthier. Just imagine a doctor telling a business to go on a diet (cut costs) and you have the right idea!

Whether through financial planning, tech upgrades, or other creative solutions, your role in an advisory team would be to help the business boost its bottom line and stay financially fit.

Oh and did we mention that you don't necessarily need an accounting degree to work in advisory? Top firms are actually hiring more and more grads from different backgrounds to build up their advisory practices.

Accounting

The accounting side of things is like a doctor taking your temperature or checking your heartbeat to make sure everything's OK.

As an accountant, you'd track and record the dollars coming in and going out - sales, expenses, taxes and more. You'll ensure the numbers add up, balancing the books and keeping a pulse on profitability.

You'd also make sure that the company follows all the necessary rules and laws about money – especially when it comes to paying their taxes!

Accountants can work:

- In-house at companies in basically any industry

- At public accounting firms, where they help client companies with their accounting needs

Now let's dive into the different types of firms.

- **The 'Big Four'**
  The Big Four accounting firms are the four huge companies that dominate the accounting scene worldwide: Deloitte, EY, KPMG, and PwC. In addition to typical audit and tax services, they also offer the widest range of advisory services in the industry. And most importantly, they hire tons of grads!

- **Mid-tier international firms**
  These companies are like the Big Four in that they're a big deal in their own right and they work all around the world. The main difference is that these mid-tier firms often focus more on mid-sized businesses, or specific industries (like manufacturing or retail).

Where are the best places to work?

Sector Rank	Employer	Location of opportunities	Accepting applications from / Types of opportunities	Learn more
#1	**Deloitte Australia** 4.2 ★★★★☆ #3 Overall	⊙ Sydney, Western Sydney, Melbourne, Perth, Brisbane, Adelaide, Canberra, Hobart, Launceston, Darwin	B C E H I L M P S T **Graduate jobs** **Internships**	Page 135
#2	**PwC Australia** 3.7 ★★★☆☆ #7 Overall	⊙ Australia	B C E H I L M P S T **Graduate jobs** **Internships**	Page 137
#3	**KPMG Australia** 3.9 ★★★★☆ #11 Overall	⊙ Sydney, Melbourne, Canberra, Brisbane, Gold Coast, Perth, Adelaide, Darwin, Hobart, Parramatta, Wollongong, Geelong, Townsville	B C E H I L M P S T **Graduate jobs** **Internships**	Page 139
#4	**BDO Australia** 4.2 ★★★★☆ #22 Overall	⊙ Perth, Sydney, Melbourne, Brisbane, Cairns, Adelaide, Hobart, Darwin	B C E H I L M P S **Graduate jobs** **Internships**	Page 144
#5	**Grant Thornton** 4.1 ★★★★☆ #27 Overall	⊙ Sydney, Melbourne, Brisbane, Adelaide, Cairns, Perth	B I L **Graduate jobs** **Internships**	Page 147

- **National firms**
  National firms have offices all around the country and they do a lot of the same stuff as the big international companies - like helping with finances, taxes, and business advice – but typically serve smaller businesses, individuals, and companies in specific areas.

- **Specialist advisory firms:** These firms offer services in really specific areas. For example, they might specialise in something like insolvency (when a company can't pay its debts).

What jobs are there?

Now we know who the big players are, let's dive into what jobs they offer and how much they pay!

Audit & assurance roles

In recent years, companies have recruited 'Audit Graduates' and 'Audit & Assurance Graduates.'

In these roles, you'd help check a company's financial records for accuracy. You might also dig deeper, examining a company's controls (the rules and procedures it has in place to prevent errors or fraud).

Tax roles

Top firms have hired for roles titled 'Tax Graduates' and 'Corporate Tax Graduates.'

You'd help clients prepare tax returns, make sure they're following the latest tax regulations, and help them prepare for future tax situations.

Consulting & advisory roles

Look for graduate programs that have words like 'consulting,' '(business) advisory,' 'corporate finance,' 'risk (management)' or 'strategy' in the name. There are also some data & tech consulting roles.

Here are a few kinds of consulting to give you an idea.

Risk is about looking at what might go wrong in a company and then helping the company prepare for it or prevent it.

Restructuring is about helping companies clean up financial messes so they can get back on their feet. You might suggest changes like cutting costs or selling company assets.

Corporate finance advisory is similar to investment banking in that they guide clients through mergers & acquisitions. The difference is that the stakes are lower (think: smaller amounts of money) and the hours are better.

Roles at top companies in order of salary

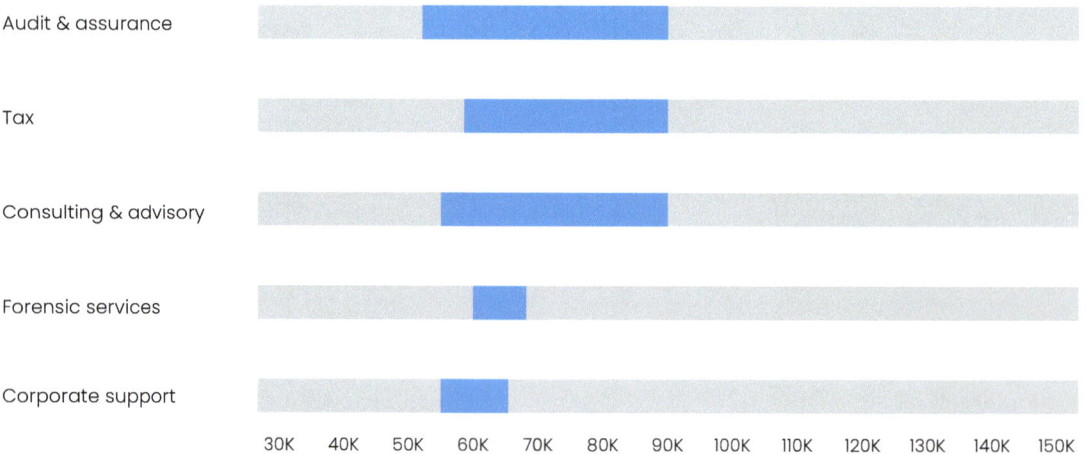

Audit & assurance	50K–90K
Tax	55K–90K
Consulting & advisory	55K–90K
Forensic services	57K–65K
Corporate support	55K–65K

30K 40K 50K 60K 70K 80K 90K 100K 110K 120K 130K 140K 150K

Is it for me?

Do I need a relevant degree?

66%
of recent grads
in this sector studied
Business & management

IT & computer science	12%
Law, legal studies & justice	7%
Sciences	6%
Engineering & mathematics	5%
Other	5%

How much would I make?

Average pay by region

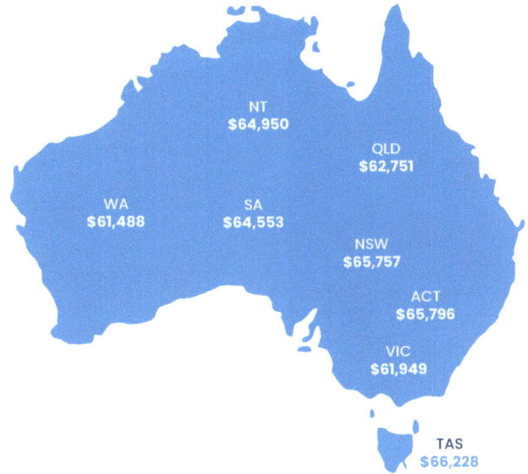

NT $64,950

QLD $62,751

WA $61,488

SA $64,553

NSW $65,757

ACT $65,796

VIC $61,949

TAS $66,228

Average salary
$57-$66K

Average hourly wage
$28.60

How much would I work each week?

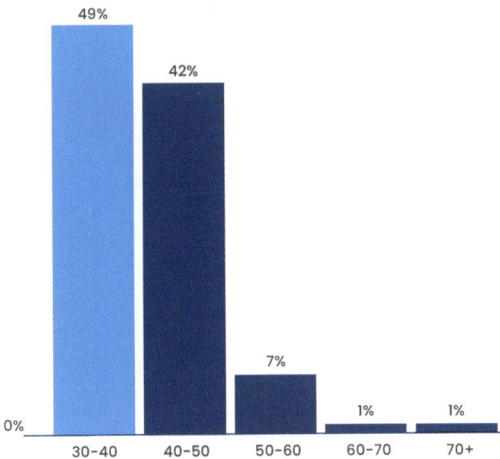

30-40	40-50	50-60	60-70	70+
49%	42%	7%	1%	1%
0%				

Would I enjoy the work?

☺ Quantity and quality of learning, training, and professional development opportunities

☺ The wide range of work and exposure to diverse clients

☺ Flexible work arrangements promoting work-life balance

☹ The stress of being in a high performing work culture

☹ Feeling like a 'cog in the wheel', doing tedious work at a large firm

☹ Salaries are relatively low

Average rating

3.9
out of
5.0

★★★★☆

On the job

Cody Rapley

Bachelor of Business
(Economics/Marketing);
Queensland University
of Technology

Consultant, Strategy
and Transactions
at EY Australia

**Building a better
working world**

'For my team specifically, we have recurring lunches and learn lectures specific to our work and dedicated transaction diligence courses for each junior level spanning two to three days. Aside from that, I also like to use EY's free access to online learning modules.'

Scan to
read more
graduate stories

Can you share insights into the mentorship or guidance you received during your journey within your team and the wider EY community?

Starting when I was a vacationer, my team was incredibly welcoming and supportive, helping to create the best experience I could have in my short internship. During the internship, my counsellor would sit down with me regularly and check in to see how I was doing. During these sessions, I would bring a big list of questions, which he would then run through with me one-by-one and make sure I understood. Many of those conversations formed the basis for what I understand today.

When I returned as a consultant, I began performing more extensive, complex tasks and whole projects. While I mentioned that this was daunting at first, I continued to have the full support of my teammates whenever I was struggling with a certain task. In addition to that, I regularly meet with my counsellor to discuss my career and what I should be focusing on to advance. Those discussions have been invaluable and have steered me forward in my career.

Outside of my team, there have been a number of other EY people who have supported me while also celebrating my culture. I am the first in my family to work in the corporate environment and one of the few Indigenous workers in the Brisbane office.

Describe a specific project or task from your early days that stands out as a valuable learning experience. How did it contribute to your professional growth?

A standout project for me would have been a due diligence project my team performed on an allied health franchise. The due diligence project was the first project I saw from beginning to end, and there were several tasks that I had not completed before. While the learning curve was steep and a bit stressful at times, I had a senior consultant alongside me, walking through anything I needed to do and ensuring I was on the right track. Overall, that project gave me my first real taste of transaction diligence and how it works.

What aspects of your job have evolved since you started, and how have you adapted with these changes?

The largest change, I would say, is growth in responsibility. At the beginning of my career, I was allocated tasks and explained how to do them, whereas now I participate in discussions on how certain projects can be approached and even give tasks to new staff.

How have you actively sought out opportunities for skill development and advancement within EY?

One of my favourite aspects of EY is that it has a culture of constant learning and growth. For my team specifically, we have recurring lunches and learn lectures specific to our work and dedicated transaction diligence courses for each junior level spanning two to three days. Aside from that, I also like to use EY's free access to online learning modules, and I am looking to begin my Chartered Accounts this year.

On the job

Melissa Bandara

Bachelor of Commerce (Accounting); Macquarie University

Climate and Engineering Graduate at Deloitte Australia

Deloitte.

'I have supported the development of innovative multi-tier risk sensing solutions and acted in an advisory capacity to explore the implications of various geo-political/economic shocks through the perspective of an automotive manufacturer.

Scan to read more graduate stories

What is your role at Deloitte and what it involves?

As a graduate of the Brisbane Climate and Engineering Consulting Team, I work closely with my team to help solve the complex business problems that our global clients face by enhancing the performance of their operations. It's exciting, challenging and scratches that part of my mind that keeps me engaged. For the past year, I have been part of a team doing multi-tier supply analysis for a major auto original equipment manufacturer.

In that role, I have supported the development of innovative multi-tier risk sensing solutions and acted in an advisory capacity to explore the implications of various geo-political/economic shocks through the perspective of an automotive manufacturer.

What work have you been most excited about since starting with us?

Working with a global automotive manufacturer has been a highlight during my grad experience. It has given me the opportunity to work on international issues such as supply exposure to the recent COVID-induced Shanghai lockdowns, with subject matter experts in supply chain resilience, innovation, industrial re-design, and data analytics.

How has the graduate program supported you in launching your career?

The Deloitte graduate program helped set me up for success from my very first day at Deloitte. The program provided a seamless transition from university life to the world of consulting. Consulting training, network opportunities and continuous support from my team were all pivotal in making my transition successful.

Moving interstate was also a big step for me, and the graduate program allowed me to meet so many like-minded individuals from different educational disciplines and business units. The colleagues I met on day one, both from my graduate cohort and my business unit, have now turned into some of my dearest and closest friends. I have so many opportunities at Deloitte, it's hard to know where to start.

What does a typical day at Deloitte look like?

By 8:00 AM I would arrive at the office and find a hot desk by the window so I can get started on checking my emails. Then I would have coffee with the Junior Team at 9:00, followed by Project Team Stand-Up. At 9:30 AM I would start working on the Project Work that involves research & story boarding.

We have a Lunch & Learn session from 12:00 to 1:00 PM, in which afterwards I continue my Project Work - this time developing the slides. Coffee catch-up with my career coach is scheduled for 2:00 PM, followed by Industrial Re-design and Innovation Community Call at 2:30 PM.

Starting from 4:00 PM I would practise the presentation of my project work and then have my slide deck reviewed. I would then wrap up the day at work by playing social netball with the team!

Banking, trading & financial services

Note: On our website, we divide this sector into two separate ones – 'Banking & financial services' and 'Trading.'

Banking

Banks play a key role in our lives – and in the economy as a whole. Here are some of the main things they do.

- First off, they provide **bank accounts** where we can store and receive money from others.

- They also provide **credit** – which is what allows us to buy things when we don't have enough money. With credit, the bank pays for us first, and then we pay them back later. Credit cards, loans, and lines of credit are some of the ways they make this possible.

- Banks can even help companies **raise money** for big projects or expansions. Imagine a company wanting to build a new factory. The bank can help them sell shares of their stocks or issue bonds to get the funds they need to make it happen.

There are two main types of banks.

- **Commercial banks** are the ones that focus on serving regular folks like us as well as small- to medium-sized businesses.

- On the other hand, **investment banks** work with big corporations, the government, and wealthy individuals, to help them tackle complex financial activities. Ever heard of IPOs? That's the work of an investment bank!

Financial services

'Financial services' usually refers to a wide range of services beyond traditional banking. For example:

- **Investment management:** This is when investment professionals take care of your money and decide where to invest it to make it grow.

- **Insurance services:** Insurance services act as a safety net to protect us from unexpected financial burdens.

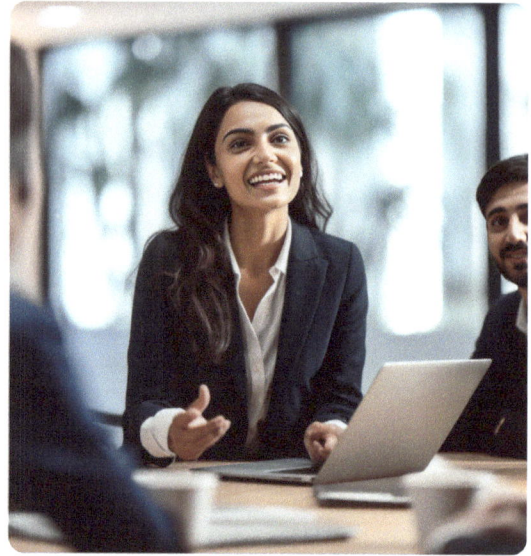

Trading

Trading is the art and science of buying and selling stuff in the financial world. Picture it as a giant marketplace where busy traders buy and sell stocks, bonds, currencies, and more.

- **Proprietary trading** or 'prop trading' is when companies use their own money to make moves in the market. Their team of expert traders studies the market, makes predictions, and decides which assets to buy or sell. If they guess right and sell at a higher price than what they bought for, they make bank.

- Instead of manually making trades, some firms use computer algorithms to analyse heaps of market data at lightning speed. Called **algorithmic trading**, this technique allows firms to pounce on even tiny price differences and make trades in a blink of an eye!

- Some trading firms call themselves **market makers**. This means they're like busy middlemen in the marketplace, always ready to buy and sell. In fact, when you buy or sell a share of a company's stock, you have traders to thank! Instead of waiting for a buyer, you can directly sell to these middlemen, who hold onto those shares until a buyer comes along.

Where are the best places to work?

Sector Rank	Employer	Location of opportunities	Accepting applications from / Types of opportunities	Learn more
Banking & financial services				
#1	**NAB Australia** 4.6 ★★★★½ #2 Overall	All over Australia, work from home	B C E H I L M P S T Graduate jobs Internships	Page 134
#2	**Commonwealth Bank** 4.4 ★★★★½ #4 Overall	Multiple locations in Australia	B C E H I L M P S T Graduate jobs Internships	Page 135
#3	**ANZ** 4.4 ★★★★½ #18 Overall	Melbourne, Sydney, Brisbane, Adelaide, Perth	B C E H I L M P S T Graduate jobs Internships	Page 142
Trading				
#1	**Optiver** 4.5 ★★★★½ #5 Overall	Sydney	B E I S Graduate jobs Internships	Page 136
#2	**IMC Trading Australia** 4.5 ★★★★½ #10 Overall	Sydney	E I S Graduate jobs Internships	Page 138
#3	**Tibra Capital** 4.1 ★★★★☆ #31 Overall	Sydney, Wollongong, London	B E I S Graduate jobs Internships	Page 149

What jobs are there?

Trading firm roles

Trading firms hire researchers, traders, and engineers.

Researchers (also known as 'quants') develop trading strategies using methods like mathematical models.

Traders are the ones who place the trades and keep a close eye on them during market hours.

Hardware and software engineers at trading firms create sophisticated systems that analyse vast amounts of data, manage risks, and execute trades with lightning speed.

Institutional & investment banking roles

Institutional and investment banking operations help big organisations like corporations and the government with their financial needs.

In institutional or corporate banking, you'd help clients manage their accounts, get loans for growing their businesses, and facilitate transactions for international trade.

In investment banking, you'd help clients raise large amounts of funding (think: IPOs) and guide them through mergers & acquisitions.

Finance & treasury roles

Finance & treasury roles are all about managing the bank's money so it grows and succeeds financially.

A bank treasury is kind of like the bank's own 'personal bank account manager'. They make sure the bank has enough cash on hand to pay its bills and take advantage of good investment opportunities. They also manage the bank's borrowing and lending to make sure the bank is financially healthy and following all the rules.

Risk & compliance roles

In risk & compliance roles, your work helps the bank minimise its potential for losses and other types of trouble.

In compliance, you'd make sure the bank is following all the rules and regulations it needs to so that it doesn't get fined or penalised.

Personal & business banking roles

In recent years, banks have recruited grads for personal & business banking programs.

In personal banking, you'd help enhance the banking experience for customers like you and me. For instance, you might help develop new products like credit cards and personal loans.

In business banking, you build relationships with business owners, understand their needs, and help them get loans to grow their business.

Tech & data roles

In a tech role, you'd develop software, manage databases, maintain networks, and digitise things.

In a data analytics role, you'd collect, process, and interpret data to help the bank make smarter decisions.

Commercial roles roles

Commercial roles include things like marketing, branding, and strategy.

Roles at top companies in order of salary

Banking & financial services

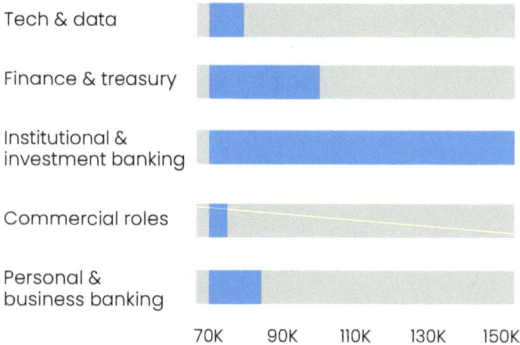

Trading

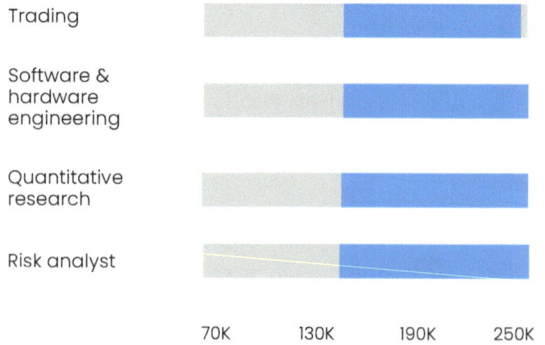

Is it for me?

Do I need a relevant degree?

Banking & financial Services

29% of recent grads in this sector studied **Business & management**

Finance, accounting, economics & business administration **20%**

Engineering & mathematics **18%**

IT & computer Science **17%**

Law, legal studies & justice **6%**

Other **10%**

Trading

43% of recent grads in this sector studied **Engineering & mathematics**

IT & computer science **30%**

Business & management **13%**

Sciences **9%**

Other **6%**

How much would I work each week?

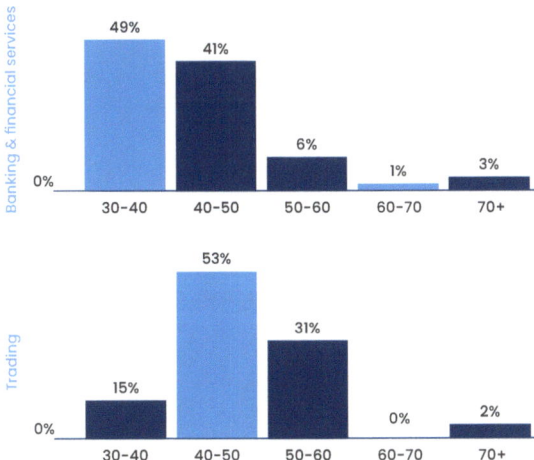

Banking & financial services

- 30-40: 49%
- 40-50: 41%
- 50-60: 6%
- 60-70: 1%
- 70+: 3%

Trading

- 30-40: 15%
- 40-50: 53%
- 50-60: 31%
- 60-70: 0%
- 70+: 2%

How much would I make?

Average pay by region

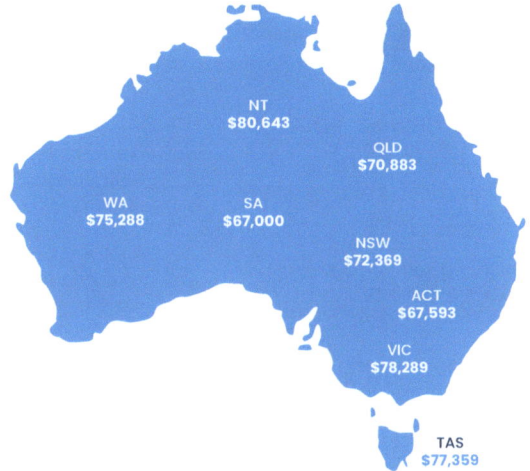

- NT $80,643
- QLD $70,883
- WA $75,288
- SA $67,000
- NSW $72,369
- ACT $67,593
- VIC $78,289
- TAS $77,359

Banking & financial services

$64–$77K Average salary

$32.50 Average hourly wage

Trading

$154–$190K Average salary

$65.87 Average hourly wage

Would I enjoy the work?

Banking & financial services

- 😊 Flexible working hours and arrangements
- 😊 Strong focus on diversity and inclusion
- 😊 Good work-life balance, exposure to different areas and teams
- ☹️ Slow moving due to the scale of the company
- ☹️ Low pay (outside of investment banking)
- ☹️ Constant corporate restructures leading to instability and uncertainty

Trading

- 😊 Opportunity to work on challenging and unique problems with smart and good people
- 😊 Generous perks and compensation
- 😊 Satisfaction of directly seeing the results of your work
- ☹️ High expectations and demanding workload
- ☹️ Long and inconsistent hours
- ☹️ Low remuneration compared to the hours and industry standards

4.4 OUT OF **5.0** ⭐⭐⭐⭐⭐ Average rating

On the job

Trina Tjugito

Bachelor of Commerce, Marketing; University of New South Wales

Consumer Graduate at Westpac Group

W GROUP

'... I assist the team with identifying and implementing uplift opportunities to better serve our customers need as well as address pain points that exist for our bankers and customers. This involves articulating what success looks like for a product and working together with a team to turn that vision into a reality.'

Explain what your business area does or their function within the group.

Consumer Banking involves everything that happens between the customer and the bank. Our objective is to optimise the customer journey process and remove customer pain points along the way.

Why did you apply for a graduate role at Westpac Group, and why your chosen business area?

I wanted to be part of a community where I can learn and grow with like-minded people with the objective of helping Australians succeed.

I joined consumer banking as this area will allow me to do so – it will provide me with the opportunity to better understand customers and in return, improve their overall experience with the bank.

To date: please provide an overview of the rotation(s) you have completed and, if cross-functional, which business areas/groups you have worked in.

My first rotation was in Customer Care. I was exposed to our front-line branch network of bankers and customers. During my time in this rotation, I helped to review the processes we have in place for our customers going through key life moments, worked with strategists to revolutionise our current processes and identify ways in which we can deliver a seamless customer journey experience.

I also worked in a product manager rotation within the Everyday Banking Line of Business. Their function is to improve our product offerings for different types of customers and assist them in building their wealth and manage their finances in better ways.

To date: has there been a project you have been involved in that you found particularly exciting or engaging?

I drove improving a reporting process within the Customer Care team which has been monumental in assisting the team in improving their efficiency and reducing their workload significantly.

So far, what has been the highlight of the graduate program?

Being involved in meaningful projects that have the potential to change and improve Australian lives has been a rewarding part of the graduate experience.

What is one thing you love about Westpac Group?

All of the people I've met have stayed within the Group for a significant amount of time. I believe this speaks about the culture of the Group – the vast range of opportunities offered within the Group means that you will always be able to grow and continuously challenge yourself!

Scan to read more **graduate stories**

Please describe your business area in three words.

Exciting, Fast-paced, Lively.

Which part of the business do you work in now?

Cash and Transactional Banking

What does your role entail?

As a product manager in the transactions team, I assist the team with identifying and implementing uplift opportunities to better serve our customers need as well as address pain points that exist for our bankers and customers. This involves articulating what success looks like for a product and working together with a team to turn that vision into a reality.

In what way did your grad program journey prepare you for your current role?

Throughout my graduate program, I was provided with the opportunity to complete a few product management rotations as well as work closely with Product Teams across the division. This gave me insights into some of the day-to-day work that

may be involved, some of the challenges that our customers and company may face, as well as the exciting opportunities that come along with it.

What are you most looking forward to?

I'm looking forward to learning more about our current offerings and how we can continue to improve our customer experience as well as drive the change to help our teams work more efficiently throughout the value chain.

What was unexpected / a surprise?

Having a fellow grad friend in my new team was a nice surprise.

Please sum up your grad experience (to date) in three words.

Welcoming, unpredictable, rewarding!

Do you have any advice for when they come to seek post-program roles?

Leverage off the networks that you have built throughout your graduate program and trust in the process.

Construction & property services

Photo courtesy of Struxture

Construction

'Construction' is all the work that goes into:

- planning, designing, and building new structures

- keeping those structures in shape

- making changes as needed

These structures could be anything from individual buildings (think: homes, offices, factories) to massive infrastructure projects (think: tunnels and dams)!

Construction involves a good amount of engineering. For instance, a construction company might need to find a way to ensure a skyscraper can withstand high winds or build a bridge over a wide river. This is why construction companies are sometimes also called 'construction & engineering firms.'

Property services

'Property services' refer to all the different kinds of work related to property. Businesses in this sector:

- buy and sell properties

- take care of properties by keeping them clean and safe

- develop properties (i.e. buy land and turn it into something that has greater value)

Where are the best places to work?

Sector Rank	Employer	Location of opportunities	Accepting applications from / Types of opportunities	Learn more
#1	**John Holland** 4.3 ★★★★☆ #45 Overall	Victoria, New South Wales, Queensland, Western Australia, Adelaide	B C E H I L M P S T Graduate jobs Internships	Page 156
#2	**Monadelphous** 4.1 ★★★★☆ #59 Overall	Brisbane, Perth	B E P S Graduate jobs Internships	Page 163
#3	**ACCIONA Australia and New Zealand** 4.2 ★★★★☆ #84 Overall	Queensland, New South Wales, Victoria, South Australia, Western Australia, New Zealand	B C E H I L M P S Graduate jobs	Page 175

The top companies in this space tend to be big property developers or construction firms. Let's take a closer look at what they do.

- **Property developers:** Developers are like the directors of a movie. They have the vision for a project, like a new building or neighbourhood, and it's their job to make it happen. This means everything from finding the money to fund the project to hiring the right professionals (like architects and construction firms). When they finish a project, they can either sell the final product or keep it and make money from it over time.

- **Construction firms:** Continuing the movie analogy, construction firms would be like the production crew. They're responsible for taking ideas (or the 'script') and turning them into real, physical structures (the 'movie'). This means managing the day-to-day work on the construction site and making sure everything is built properly, safely, and on time.

There are also companies that are both of these things combined. For example, some companies are construction firms that branched into property development and vice versa.

What jobs are there?

Engineering roles

In recent years, top construction & property companies have hired engineers in these disciplines: chemical, mechanical, mechatronic, and civil engineering.

As an entry-level engineer, you'll get to put your skills to practise in a variety of tasks from designing structures to project management and site supervision.

HSE/Sustainability roles

As a health, safety, and environment (HSE) officer, your job is to protect workers, the public, and the environment from harm by visiting construction sites and making sure they comply with relevant regulations.

Sustainability roles are more varied – you might get to work on a business case for green initiatives or help compile a list of endangered species on development sites.

Property development roles

In a property development role, you'll get exposure to key parts of the development process and possibly different types of developments as well (e.g. retirement villages if you're on a residential property team and shopping centres if you're on a commercial property team).

You might get to work on pricing and competitor analysis, meet with tenants who are leasing your company's properties, and visit sites to stay up-to-date on construction progress.

Investment management roles

Many property developers also provide investment management services – which is when you invest a client's funds for them to help them make money.

As an investment manager at a property developer, you would help clients (like pension funds and insurance companies) invest in property, allowing them to diversify their portfolios and generate stable long-term returns.

Construction management roles

Construction management roles are on the lower end of the salaries in this sector.

Construction management graduates steer construction projects from planning to completion, manage budgets, enforce safety protocols, and keep stakeholders in the loop.

Corporate support roles

In recent years, construction & property companies have hired graduates for their HR, IT, and accounting departments.

Roles at top companies in order of salary

Here are the jobs that the top-ranked companies have posted on our site and how much they pay.

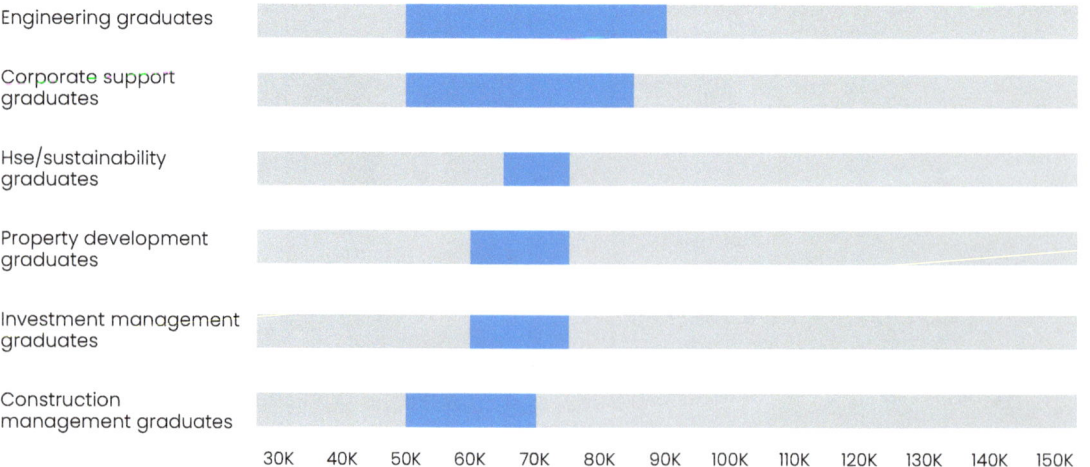

Is it for me?

Do I need a relevant degree?

55%
of recent grads
in this sector studied
Engineering & mathematics

Property & built environment	**14%**
IT & computer sciences	**12%**
Business & management	**9%**
Sciences	**5%**
Other	**4%**

How much would I make?

Average pay by region

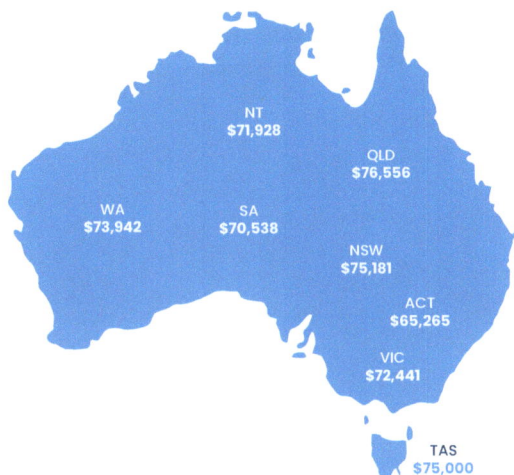

NT $71,928

QLD $76,556

WA $73,942

SA $70,538

NSW $75,181

ACT $65,265

VIC $72,441

TAS $75,000

Average salary
$61-$74K

Average hourly wage
$26.91

How much would I work each week?

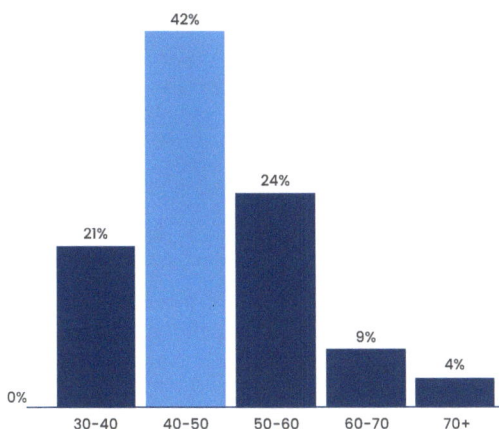

Hours	Percentage
30–40	21%
40–50	42%
50–60	24%
60–70	9%
70+	4%

Would I enjoy the work?

☺ Exposure to a wide range of projects and sectors
☺ Exciting projects like high-profile, landmark projects or large-scale infrastructure projects.
☺ Opportunities for travel and site visits
☹ Rigid bureaucracy and lots of red tape
☹ Outdated technology systems
☹ Long working hours, including overtime and weekend shifts

Average rating

4.1
out of
5.0

★★★★☆

On the job

James Dowzard

Bachelor of Engineering
(Mechatronic Engineering);
University of New South Wales

Rail Graduate
at John Holland

**JOHN
HOLLAND**

'My work is office-based so depending on where the project is, I am usually involved in developing a report to make an assurance argument, or another key report I worked on was to demonstrate that the design was capable of meeting its high-level targets for trains running on time.'

Provide an overview of all your rotations to date:

For the past two years I have worked on Sydney Metro Northwest delivering the Operations, Trains and Systems Package (worth around $3 billion).

What does your typical workday look like?

My day will usually start with some planning. I always like to have goals for my day in terms of what I want to achieve.

My work is office-based so depending on where the project is, I am usually involved in developing a report to make an assurance argument, or another key report I worked on was to demonstrate that the design was capable of meeting its high-level targets for trains running on time.

I also assist in other areas of the systems engineering team such as requirements, usually writing scripts to automate some of the processes we need to execute as a project. Programming is an extremely useful way to remove the need for manual processes and enable our project team to utilise their specific expertise more often throughout the day.

What has been the most interesting thing about your job?

The exposure to the largest public-private partnership is something I have come more recently to appreciate.

What keeps the work I do interesting is that the project lifecycle always moves forward, meaning you are always working towards a huge milestone – completing the project, which then brings benefit to the communities we work in.

What are the limitations of your role?

Being a graduate can be seen as a limitation, however, I use it as an opportunity to ask lots of questions and learn a lot from people with a lot of experience.

What is something you wish you knew before you started?

To back yourself more. It is easy to stand off a bit when working with people with over 30 years' experience. More and more though, I have come to back myself and just see it as a level playing field, which has reaped rewards for me.

How did you prepare for starting on the Graduate Program?

I went to South America for a month! Before this program, I had worked with John Holland for a year as an undergraduate so for me, I was comfortable entering the program.

Scan to
read more
graduate stories

On the job

Brittney Monk

Bachelor of Engineering (Civic); University of New South Wales

Graduate Engineer at Acciona Australia and New Zealand

acciona

'There is a lot of planning that goes into construction works and although I find this enjoyable the best part of the job is when you are actually out on-site watching everything come together.'

What's your job about?

I am currently working in the construction engineering team at Burwood North Station on the Sydney Metro West – Central Tunnelling Package.

What's your background?

I was in Year 12 when I attended the UNSW Women In Engineering Camp, and that's when I truly decided that engineering was the path for me. After this camp, I was set on working as an engineer in transport planning (working in construction wasn't even on my radar).

Before starting uni, I was awarded a scholarship sponsored by Transurban where I then went on to work part-time for 4 years while I completed my degree. Although I loved uni, this work experience is where I learnt the most and where I discovered my love for construction. I worked at WestConnex 3A for 2.5 years on the client side and found myself getting jealous of those engineers who were working on site all the time. This is what led me to apply for a position at Acciona.

Could someone with a different background do your job?

An engineering degree is imperative to my job – although I don't use every part of my degree every day, the knowledge you gain from a civil engineering degree is key to understanding each activity on site.

What's the coolest thing about your job?

I don't think there are many jobs where you can watch something go from paper to a huge structure every single day. There is a lot of planning that goes into construction works and although I find this enjoyable the best part of the job is when you are actually out on-site watching everything come together.

What are the limitations of your job?

As much as I love my job, sometimes it feels like there really isn't a lot of time for anything else. These long hours can be exhausting and really limit the amount of time you have to spend with family and friends. This is by far the biggest downside of the job.

3 pieces of advice for yourself when you were a student...

- Apply for every opportunity – even if you don't 100% meet the criteria or think it might be out of your comfort zone, do it anyway!

- You don't always have to have a plan – I had my whole degree planned out from the first year and I had a million curve balls thrown at me. At first, I was annoyed that things didn't go exactly to plan but looking back I am glad they turned out the way they did.

- Always make time for yourself – it is more important to be refreshed and work effectively than burn yourself out.

Scan to read more **graduate stories**

Defence, R&D & manufacturing

Note: On our website, this sector is broken up into two separate sectors: 'Defence & aerospace' and 'R&D & manufacturing.'

R&D & manufacturing

This sector drives the creation of a wide range of goods that enhance our lives—from life-saving medicines and cutting-edge electronics to efficient vehicles and everyday consumer goods. Here's how it works:

1. **R&D (Research & Development):** First up is R&D – the process of inventing new products or improving existing ones through research and testing.

2. **Design:** This is the process of creating the blueprints or plans for a product that works properly, looks good, and is easy to make in large quantities.

3. **Manufacturing:** The real magic happens on the factory floor where raw materials are transformed into finished products.

4. **Quality control:** Finished products are inspected, tested, and sampled to make sure that everything leaving the factory works as promised.

5. **Packaging & distribution:** This is when products are prepared for delivery and then shipped to wherever they need to be!

Depending on their relative strengths and weaknesses, different countries specialise in different parts of the process:

- Countries like Australia and New Zealand do a lot more R&D than manufacturing and the manufacturing that does happen occurs in more niche and specialised areas – think: medical devices instead of consumer goods like clothes and cars.

- On the other hand, countries like the Philippines and Indonesia focus more on the manufacturing side of things. Given their large labour forces and competitive labour costs, these countries excel in mass-producing consumer goods. However, they're also working to beef up their R&D skills, especially in areas like electronics and biotechnology.

Photo courtesy of SAAB Australia

Defence & aerospace

This may seem like an oddly specific sector to single out, but quite a few companies in this space have made it onto our top 100 list, highlighting its popularity with grads.

Here's a glimpse into what this sector does and what they're known for:

- **Weapons manufacturing:** Companies in this space design, develop, produce, maintain, and support defence and aerospace equipment, systems, and technologies.

- **Cybersecurity:** An indispensable part of modern defence systems, cybersecurity providers protect sensitive data, and tackle evolving cyber threats.

- **Exports:** Australia's defence industry has been successful in exporting internationally. For example, 70+ Australian companies are responsible for making the components of the F-35 – one of the most advanced fighter jets in the world.

By the way, companies in this sector are often called 'defence contractors.' That's because governments hire them (give them contracts to) to do defence-related work. And because they're granted long-term contracts from the government, they offer a high level of stability and sustained growth opportunities.

Where are the best places to work?

Sector Rank	Employer	Location of opportunities	Accepting applications from / Types of opportunities	Learn more

R&D and manufacturing

| #1 | CSIRO 4.4 ★★★★☆ #63 Overall | ⊙ Australian Capital Territory, New South Wales, Northern Territory, Queensland, South Australia, Tasmania, Victoria, Western Australia | B C E H I L M P S T Graduate jobs Internships | Page 165 |

Defence & aerospace

#1	BAE Systems 3.9 ★★★★☆ #34 Overall	⊙ Adelaide, Melbourne, Sydney, Newcastle, Canberra, Perth	B C E H I L M S T Graduate jobs Internships	Page 150
#2	Nova Systems 3.8 ★★★★☆ #60 Overall	⊙ Adelaide	B C E I M S Graduate jobs Internships	Page 163
#3	Boeing Australia 4.3 ★★★★☆ #61 Overall	⊙ Australian Capital Territory, New South Wales, Northern Territory, Queensland, South Australia, Victoria, Western Australia	B E I L S Graduate jobs Internships	Page 164
#4	Lockheed Martin 4.0 ★★★★☆ #83 Overall	⊙ Adelaide, Canberra	B E H I S L T Graduate jobs Internships	Page 175
#5	Leidos Australia 4.1 ★★★★☆ #89 Overall	⊙ Melbourne, Canberra	B C E H I L S T Graduate jobs Internships	Page 178

What jobs are there?

Engineering roles

In recent years, firms have hired graduates for aerospace, maritime, and civil engineering roles.

As an engineer in this field, you'd get to tinker with new ideas, create prototypes, run tests, analyse the data from those tests … all while making sure products meet both local and international rules and safety standards.

Tech & data roles

Because of the large number of defence firms, this sector has a good amount of data & tech roles, especially in software, systems, and cybersecurity engineering.

Software engineers do roughly the same stuff as in other sectors – expect to spend most of your day coding, debugging, testing, and reviewing code.

Systems engineers design and build complex hardware, software, and network systems. You might also work on integrating multiple systems into a larger, more complex system with functions ranging from communications to electronic warfare.

Cybersecurity specialists work to protect everything from cyber threats, for example by working with software engineers to build security into applications from the start.

Logistics & supply chain roles

In recent years, logistics support engineers and supply chain graduates.

In logistics & supply chain, you'd help keep everything running smoothly in a manufacturing operation, from sourcing of raw materials to delivery of the final product.

Without your expertise, the manufacturing process would face costly delays, inefficiencies, and quality control issues.

Commercial & corporate support roles

Depending on the company, you might take on commercial roles like project management, contract negotiation, and business analysis.

In recent years, companies have hired graduates for accounting & finance roles and for general graduate programs that cover a wide range of support functions from HR to compliance.

Roles at top companies in order of salary

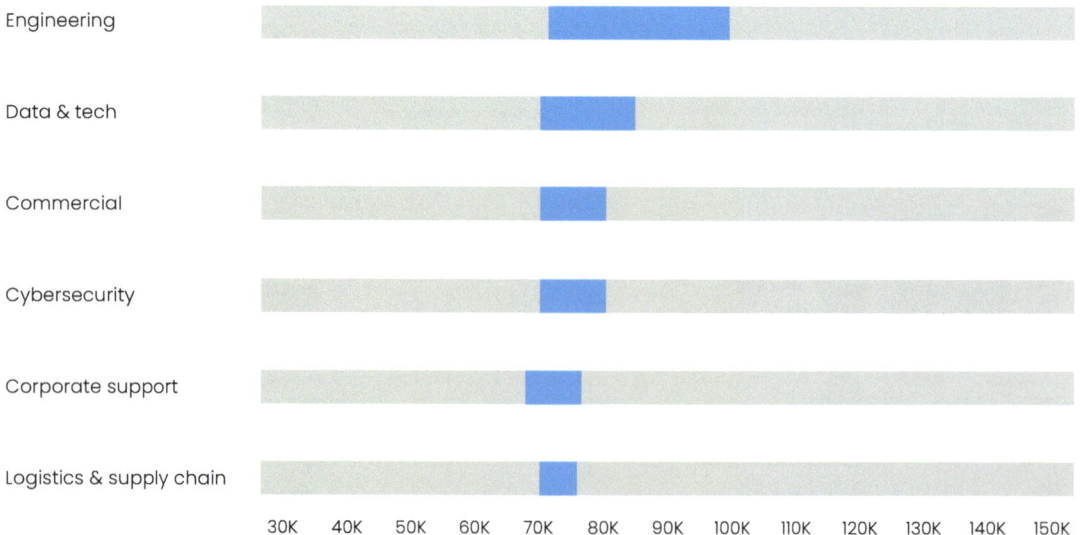

Role	Salary range
Engineering	70K–100K
Data & tech	70K–80K
Commercial	70K–78K
Cybersecurity	70K–78K
Corporate support	65K–75K
Logistics & supply chain	70K–75K

Salary axis: 30K 40K 50K 60K 70K 80K 90K 100K 110K 120K 130K 140K 150K

Is it for me?

Do I need a relevant degree?

R&D & manufacturing

52% of recent grads in this sector studied **Engineering & mathematics**

IT & computer Science **27%**

Business & management **12%**

Other **9%**

Defence & aerospace

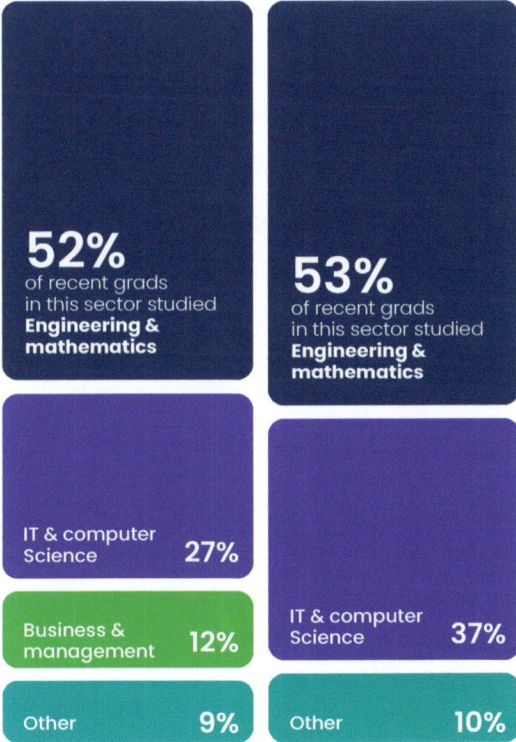

53% of recent grads in this sector studied **Engineering & mathematics**

IT & computer Science **37%**

Other **10%**

How much would I work each week?

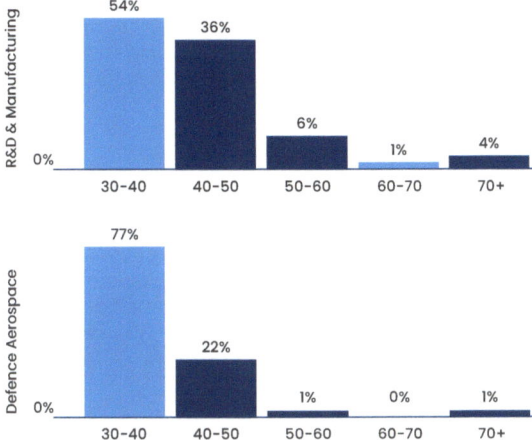

R&D & Manufacturing

- 30–40: 54%
- 40–50: 36%
- 50–60: 6%
- 60–70: 1%
- 70+: 4%

Defence Aerospace

- 30–40: 77%
- 40–50: 22%
- 50–60: 1%
- 60–70: 0%
- 70+: 1%

How much would I make?

Average pay by region

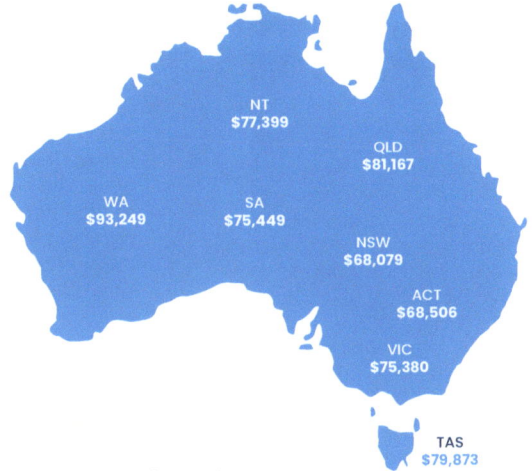

- NT $77,399
- QLD $81,167
- WA $93,249
- SA $75,449
- NSW $68,079
- ACT $68,506
- VIC $75,380
- TAS $79,873

R&D & manufacturing
$62–$80K Average salary
$31.37 Average hourly wage

Defence & aerospace
$70–$77K Average salary
$36.94 Average hourly wage

Would I enjoy the work?

R&D & manufacturing

- ☺ Supportive and friendly work environment
- ☺ Emphasis on employee happiness and work-life balance
- ☺ Exposure to senior stakeholders and opportunity to ideate and implement ideas
- ☹ Difficulty in transitioning from university skills to a working role
- ☹ Lack of structured training programs and inductions
- ☹ Lack of uniformity in processes and systems across business units

Defence & aerospace

- ☺ The opportunity to work on significant platforms/ systems/projects for Defense
- ☺ Meaningful, challenging, and exciting work
- ☺ Flexibility in regard to working start/finish times
- ☹ Longer project timelines due to extensive documentation requirements
- ☹ Limited design work
- ☹ Limited exposure to different engineering work

4.3 OUT OF **5.0** ★★★★½ Average rating

On the job

Jason Huynh

Bachelor of Engineering
(Honours) (Mechanical and
Aerospace) and Bachelor of
Mathematical and Computer
Sciences, Computer Science
Major; University of Adelaide

Graduate Aerospace
Engineer at BAE Systems

BAE SYSTEMS

'My role at BAE Systems
Australia as a graduate
aerospace engineer
primarily involves
rocket development,
simulation and
modelling. I've worked
with my team and our
customer to understand
the desired capabilities
of the rocket to be
developed and to
elicit measureable
requirements for
the engineered
components of the
rocket.'

Scan to
read more
graduate stories

What's your job about?

BAE Systems Australia is a defence and security company with
capabilities spanning the breadth of the product lifecycle. My
role at BAE Systems Australia as a graduate aerospace engineer
primarily involves rocket development, simulation and modelling.
I've worked with my team and our customer to understand the
desired capabilities of the rocket to be developed and to elicit
measureable requirements for the engineered components of the
rocket. These requirements are crucial throughout the design phase
of the project where the use of rocket modelling and simulation
is applied to rapidly evaluate rocket component configurations
against the target requirements. I've had opportunities to work with
another graduate engineer on this project and to also collaborate
with other engineers at various levels of seniority.

What's your background?

I grew up in Adelaide and studied aerospace engineering and
computer science at the University of Adelaide. Throughout uni,
I sought as much engineering experience as I could. I tutored in
a few first-year engineering courses, which was a great way to
reinforce the engineering fundamentals as well as it simply being
a gratifying experience. I did a summer research project with an
academic at uni on controlling micro-scale fluid flows for medical
applications, and also got some hands-on engineering experience
through designing a rocket with a team for the Australian
Universities Rocket Competition. Along the way, I also volunteered
for a few societies and organisations.

During my final two years of uni, I worked with multirotor drones
and Internet of Things payload devices on a part-time basis as
a cadet at Defence Science Technology Group (DSTG). I was
fortunate to be able to bring some of this work to uni as my final
year honours project which I completed with two of my mates.
As much fun as it was to build and fly a hexacopter drone and
payload from scratch, I realised I wanted to expose myself to a
greater breadth of the project lifecycle. I acknowledged that the
novelty inherent to research and development activities really
appealed to me, however, I was sorely lacking in experience across
the span of technology readiness levels. After having some candid
conversations with my cherished mentors at DSTG, I decided that
BAE Systems Australia could offer me the best opportunity for
growth.

Could someone with a different background do your job?

A job in rocket simulation and modelling requires solid foundational
skills in maths, programming, physics, and of course, engineering.
Problem-solving is the skill that ties these disciplines together,
hence, someone with a university background in STEM could handle
this job. Such a person would be able to apply their learned ways
of thinking and develop their discipline-specific skills on the job. I
certainly needed to, and continue to, bolster some of my skills to get
the job done properly and efficiently!

What's the coolest thing about your job?

I feel immensely privileged to be able to work with rockets. Rockets are among the fastest travelling vehicles ever created and are the only reliable option for space access, for now at least. Considering my fascination with research and development, it's easy to see how rockets, with their peerless capabilities, are a vector for further novel inventions!

What are the limitations of your job?

The biggest limitation of my job is the accordingly secretive nature of defence work. A consequence of this is that it's often difficult to fully grasp the details of projects happening outside of those I normally interact with. This may lead to situations where people may not know of interesting work happening elsewhere and could miss opportunities to get involved. It's generally best to simply talk to people about their work and acknowledge that there are limits on how much they can disclose.

3 pieces of advice for yourself when you were a student...

- Seek work experience opportunities coordinated by academic staff within your uni. These programs generally don't require prior experience within your field and are a great way to begin developing your professional network. Hopefully your supervisor agrees to be your referee for your future internship or full-time job applications.

- Keep an eye on the bigger picture by reading news related to industries you're interested in. It's an easy and immediate source of motivation for when you get bogged down in the minutiae of seemingly endless assignments.

- As long as your grades are decent, your mindset and behaviours matter more to employers.

Engineering consulting

Engineering consulting services help turn ideas into real, functional, and successful projects. For example:

- Imagine a city is planning to construct a new suspension bridge. They've got a basic plan, but are unsure of some details and complexities. In this case, they might hire engineering consultants to map out and design the bridge down to the smallest detail, ensuring its structure is 100% sound.

- Or suppose a car company has a prototype for an innovative electric car, but they're stuck on how to enhance its efficiency. They might bring in consultants to help evaluate the car's design, fine-tuning elements for optimal efficiency and safety.

- Or let's say a utility company wants to harness the power of the wind by building a wind farm, but isn't sure of the best locations or designs. Here, engineering consultants might use sophisticated models to identify the windiest, most suitable spots for a wind farm and suggest the most efficient turbine designs.

Along the way, they might also identify potential hurdles, offering solutions before these become real problems.

Where are the best places to work?

Sector Rank	Employer	Location of opportunities	Accepting applications from / Types of opportunities	Learn more
#1	**Arup** 4.7 ★★★★★ #9 Overall	Adelaide, Canberra, Melbourne Maroochydore, Perth, Sydney, Brisbane, Gold Coast, Cairns, Townsville, Canberra, Sunshine Coast	B E H I M P S T Graduate jobs Internships	Page 138
#2	**GHD** 3.9 ★★★★☆ #13 Overall	Australian Capital Territory, New South Wales, Northern Territory, Queensland, South Australia, Tasmania, Victoria, Western Australia	B C E H I L M P S T Graduate jobs Internships	Page 140
#3	**WSP Australia** 4.2 ★★★★☆ #16 Overall	Australia wide	B E H I L M P S Graduate jobs Internships	Page 141
#4	**Jacobs Australia** 4.1 ★★★★☆ #28 Overall	Sydney, Newcastle, Melbourne, Hobart, Adelaide, Perth, Darwin, Cairns, Townsville, Brisbane, Auckland, Christchurch, Wellington	B C E H I L M P S T Graduate jobs Internships	Page 147
#5	**Aurecon Australia** 4.1 ★★★★☆ #48 Overall	Adelaide, Brisbane, Cairns, Canberra, Darwin, Gladstone, Gold Coast, Mackay, Maroochydore, Melbourne, Newcastle, Perth, Sydney, Toowoomb	B C E H I L M P S T Graduate jobs Internships	Page 157

The engineering consulting industry is made up of many different companies, from small firms that specialise in a specific area, to large international corporations that cover many different fields of engineering.

The best ones – i.e. the ones on our Top 100 list – all have strong reputations in the industry as well as, a global footprint.

What jobs are there?

Engineering roles

In recent years, engineering consulting firms have hired engineers from disciplines such as civil, mechanical, geotechnical, materials, and chemical engineering.

Depending on your area of expertise, you might help design anything from heating systems to large-scale infrastructure. Or you might ensure that the foundations of a structure are safe or that a new bridge uses the right type of steel.

Surveying roles

Firms have also hired graduate surveyors and geo-spatial engineers.

These roles are responsible for mapping out the landscape of the project site so that construction projects can be planned and carried out.

Architecture & urban planning roles

In recent years, firms have hired graduates in architecture, landscape design, urban planning, built environment, and transport planning.

Depending on your role, you might design buildings, outdoor spaces (like parks and campuses, towns and cities, and transport systems. Or you might use your expertise to guide policies on all of the above!

Sustainability & environmental roles

In recent years, firms have hired grads for their sustainability & environmental consultant, environmental scientist, and even botanist roles.

You might evaluate the environmental impact of a client's project, assess sites for contamination, or help design green spaces that support local biodiversity.

Commercial roles

In recent years, firms have hired graduates for marketing, communications, and other unspecified commercial roles.

Roles at top companies in order of salary

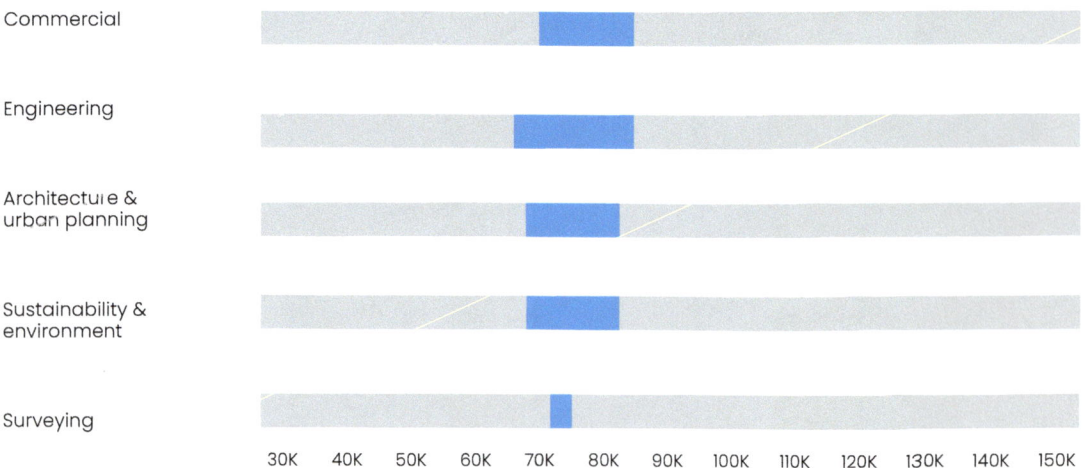

Role	Salary range
Commercial	
Engineering	
Architecture & urban planning	
Sustainability & environment	
Surveying	

30K 40K 50K 60K 70K 80K 90K 100K 110K 120K 130K 140K 150K

Is it for me?

Do I need a relevant degree?

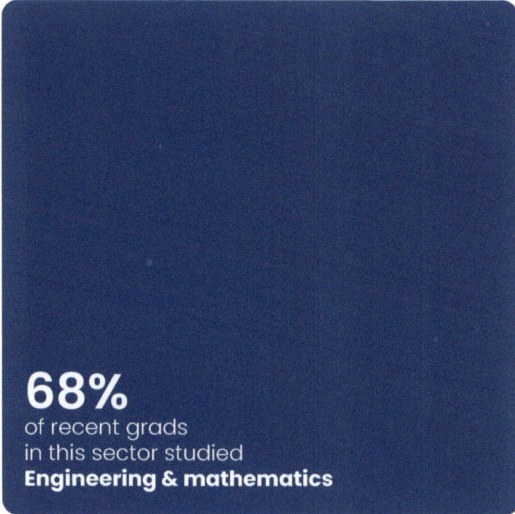

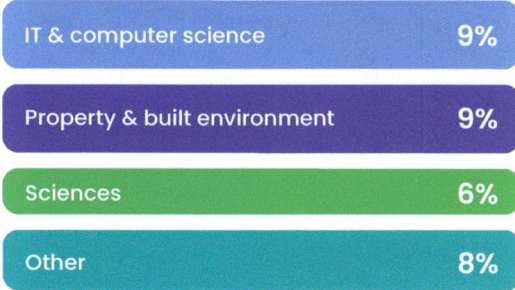

68%
of recent grads
in this sector studied
Engineering & mathematics

IT & computer science	9%
Property & built environment	9%
Sciences	6%
Other	8%

How much would I make?

Average pay by region

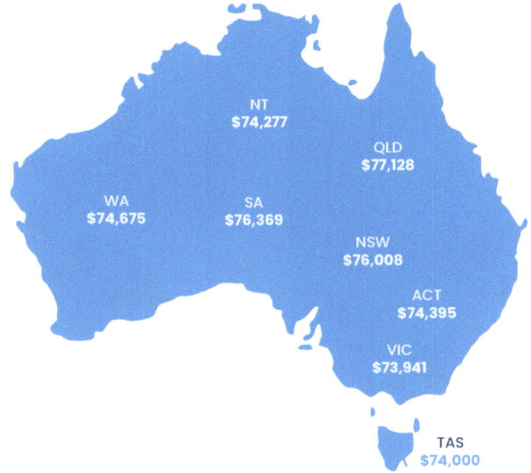

NT
$74,277

QLD
$77,128

WA
$74,675

SA
$76,369

NSW
$76,008

ACT
$74,395

VIC
$73,941

TAS
$74,000

Average salary
$68–$75K

Average hourly wage
$34.40

How much would I work each week?

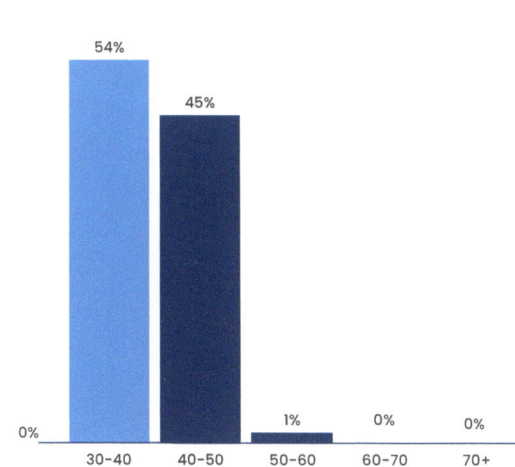

54% — 30-40
45% — 40-50
1% — 50-60
0% — 60-70
0% — 70+
0% baseline

Would I enjoy the work?

☺ Exposure to diverse range of projects
☺ Variety of global work opportunities
☺ Inclusive and respectful work environment
☹ Fluctuating work hours due to project-based work
☹ Lack of opportunities for career growth and development
☹ Lack of clarity on expectations

Average rating

4.1 out of 5.0

★★★★☆

On the job

Tess McGahan

Bachelor of Science
(Environmental Science)
& Bachelor of Laws - LLB,
Honours; Queensland
University of Technology

Graduate Consultant
at Arup

ARUP

'Over the last year,
I've been working
on an offshore wind
farm project, if
constructed it will
be one of Australia's
first-ever offshore
wind farms... It's
exciting to be ahead
of the curve and
progress renewable
energy in Australia.
So, it's great to be at
the forefront of this
technology.'

Tess is a Graduate Consultant working in our environment team in Brisbane. As a kid growing up in Central Queensland, Tess could be found hanging outside in nature, playing in the creek with friends and riding her bike along the local BMX tracks. Her love of the outdoors helped her choose a career in environmental science.

Tess best aligns with the United Nation's Sustainable Development Goal is number 15, 'Life on Land'. Learn how Arup is helping Tess create a pathway to her purpose:

Why did you choose the Arup graduate programme?

I knew a few people that worked at Arup, and they always spoke highly of the firm. The culture seemed like the right fit for me. When I was looking for opportunities, Arup was one of the only engineering companies that anchor all their work to sustainable development and had a dedicated environmental team. So, I started my journey through the vacation programme, and I knew it was a place where I could follow my purpose and take my career where I wanted it to go.

What do you get up to in your day-to-day role?

I help our clients manage environmental risks that threaten people, our cities and the environment. I've been working on significant infrastructure projects and smaller projects like environmental assessments over the last two years. In my team, we work with specialists to understand the different aspects of the environment and all the various constraints assessed for a project. In addition, I get involved in a wide range of activities, from advising policy to helping protect endangered species.

Over the last year, I've been working on an offshore wind farm project. If constructed, it will be one of Australia's first-ever offshore wind farms. The project involves conducting environmental assessments, meeting with government and community stakeholders about project approval, and working with the client to guide design decisions. It's exciting to be ahead of the curve and progress renewable energy in Australia. So, it's great to be at the forefront of this technology.

What are your future aspirations?

I want to help protect and restore our environment and mitigate impacts from climate change in the future. Continuing my work in the renewable energy space on projects like Australis will help me reach this goal. It excites me to imagine what I will be doing in the future if I'm doing such exciting work now.

Scan to
read more
graduate stories

On the job

Michael Cross

Bachelor of Science
(Geology/Earth Science);
University of Newcastle

Graduate Engineering
Geologist at WSP Australia

WSP

'You get to work with different people all the time from all walks of life. You get to see locations that few people see or are inaccessible to the public.'

How did you get to your current job position?

I had just gotten out of a long-term relationship, very abruptly, and decided I needed a change. My role as a Geotechnician wasn't stimulating enough for me and there was no further opportunity to grow in that company anytime soon. I had contacted my now current boss Jamie Anderson about a year earlier chasing a job which at the time was with Parsons Brinkerhoff which was undergoing a lot of changes becoming WSP. At this point in my life, I knew this time was different. Toward the end of the year, I was chasing up Jamie every week until I finally got an interview. A couple of months later, I acquired my job at WSP as a Graduate Engineering Geologist.

How did you choose your specialisation?

I originally thought I was applying for a Geotechnical Engineering position, but my current boss thought I would be more suited to the role of an Engineering Geologist based on my earth science background.

What are your areas of responsibility?

Geotech investigation and field testing, design, site supervision, 3D geological modelling, soil and core logging, liaising with clients and subcontractors, reporting, proposal writing, and project set up.

Can you describe a typical workday?

I do a lot of fieldwork. Typically, 75% of the time I am out in the field undertaking geotechnical investigations. I have done geotechnical fieldwork on numerous projects. Mine and dam expansion projects, Burrawang to Avon Tunnel (BAT), mine subsidence investigations, and Sydney Trains drainage investigations.

What are the career prospects with your job?

I am looking to move into project management; however, I am still enjoying doing fieldwork and hope to balance both aspects.

What do you love the most about your job?

I love being out in the field. You get to work with different people all the time from all walks of life. You get to see locations that few people see or are inaccessible to the public. Especially working in the southern highlands on the BAT project, I got to see a beautiful part of Australia that I likely wouldn't have gone to. I feel like I am constantly learning and testing myself when I'm out in the field. I also enjoy being in the office. It's a good change sometimes. It is also in a beautiful location right near Newcastle beach.

What's the biggest limitation of your job?

As much as I do love fieldwork, it means that I spend a lot of time away from home which impacts my ability to do sport and train throughout the week. Stress can sometimes be reflected when budgets and timeframes are restraining.

Government & public service

From schools to hospitals, parks to public transportation, the public sector is a big part of our daily lives. Here's a brief look at all the work they do.

Delivering essential services

The public sector provides essential services that would not be available if they were not funded by the government. For example:

- The public sector protects the country from foreign threats, builds infrastructure, and provides public healthcare to those in need.

- In many countries, the government (or government-run companies) are also responsible for providing public utilities like electricity, gas, and water.

Developing policies

The government conducts research and analyses data to come up with policies for tackling important issues, such as economic growth, social welfare, environmental protection, innovation, national security, and international relations.

Supporting government functions

An organisation as large as the government needs a lot of people working behind the scenes to keep everything running smoothly. That's why there are:

- Finance professionals who handle budgets, track expenses, ensure financial compliance.

- Communications professionals who convey important government updates and information to the media and the public.

- IT and Technology specialists who manage computer systems, networks, and software applications.

Where are the best places to work?

Sector Rank	Employer	Location of opportunities	Accepting applications from / Types of opportunities	Learn more
#1	**NSW Government** 3.9 ★★★★☆ #23 Overall	⦿ Sydney	B C E H I L M P S T Graduate jobs Internships	Page 145
#2	**Department of Defence** 4.1 ★★★★☆ #33 Overall	⦿ Adelaide, Brisbane, Canberra, Cairns, Darwin, Melbourne, Newcastle, Perth, Sydney	B C E H I L M P S T Graduate jobs Internships	Page 150
#3	**Australian Security Intelligence Organisation (ASIO)** #42 Overall	⦿ Canberra	B C E H I L M P S T Graduate jobs	Page 154
#4	**Queensland Government** 4.2 ★★★★☆ #43 Overall	⦿ Queensland	B C E H I L M P S T Graduate jobs	Page 155
#5	**Australian Taxation Office (ATO)** 4.2 ★★★★☆ #62 Overall	⦿ Adelaide, Albury, Brisbane, Canberra, Geelong, Gosford, Hobart, Melbourne, Newcastle, Perth, Sydney, Townsville, Wollongong	B C E H I L M P S T Graduate jobs	Page 164

The top employers in this space generally fall into the following categories.

- **Government agencies:** These are specific departments within the government, each responsible for particular areas such as transport, health, environment, or law enforcement.

- **Local and regional governments:** These include city, council, and regional bodies that manage local services, community planning, and development initiatives.

What jobs are there?

Legal roles

In recent years, all government agencies on our Top 100 list have hired law graduates.

In a legal role, you'd use your skills and expertise to advise on new policies, work out contracts with suppliers, and solve legal problems in areas like healthcare, construction, and defence.

Your work would play a vital role in ensuring that government actions and decisions are legally sound.

Communications roles

In recent years, government agencies have hired grads for numerous communications roles.

In communications, you'd keep the public informed, engaged, and aware of important matters that affect their lives, health, safety, and well-being.

Effective communication fosters transparency, builds trust, and encourages public participation in the decision-making processes.

Engineering & infrastructure roles

In recent years, the government has hired lots of graduates, mostly engineers, to help with big infrastructure projects and defence work – with some roles also open to humanities, arts, or social sciences students.

You could end up doing all kinds of important work from aerospace research to managing huge construction projects.

Your work would contribute to efforts to build up the country and keep it safe.

Corporate support roles

Last but not least, the government has also hired a handful of corporate support roles. Most of these have been in HR, accounting & finance.

Tech & data roles

In recent years, government agencies have hired grads for IT and data-related graduate programs.

In a data & tech role, you'd get to do things like maintain government IT systems and analyse data to improve government services.

These roles ensure that government services are accessible, data is protected, and decisions are based on accurate information.

Roles at top companies in order of salary

Here are the jobs that the top-ranked companies have posted on our site and how much they pay.

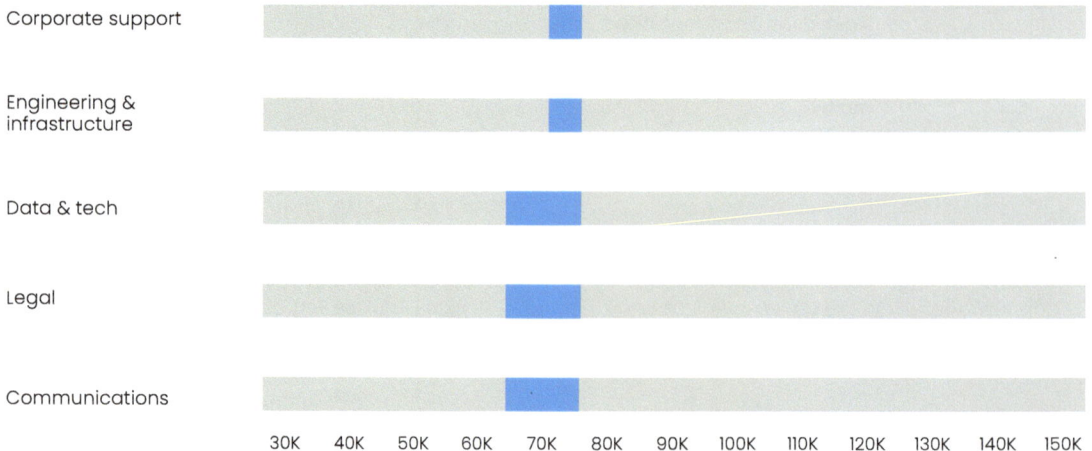

Role	Salary range
Corporate support	~70K
Engineering & infrastructure	~70K
Data & tech	~70K
Legal	~70K
Communications	~70K

30K 40K 50K 60K 70K 80K 90K 100K 110K 120K 130K 140K 150K

Is it for me?

Do I need a relevant degree?

24%
of recent grads
in this sector studied
Engineering & mathematics

Business & management	**15%**
Humanities, arts & social sciences	**14%**
Sciences	**13%**
IT & computer science	**12%**
Law, legal studies & justice	**11%**
Other	**11%**

How much would I make?

Average pay by region

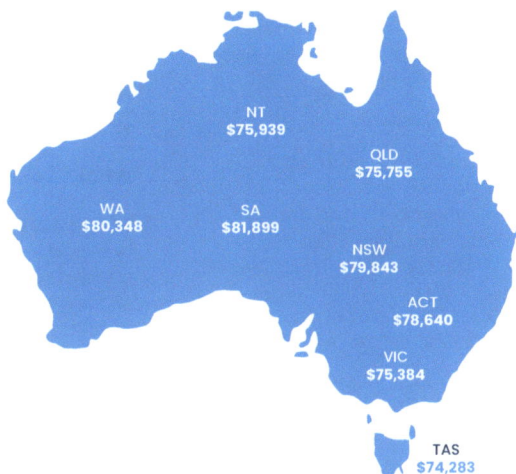

NT $75,939
QLD $75,755
WA $80,348
SA $81,899
NSW $79,843
ACT $78,640
VIC $75,384
TAS $74,283

Average salary
$70–$78K

Average hourly wage
$36.92

How much would I work each week?

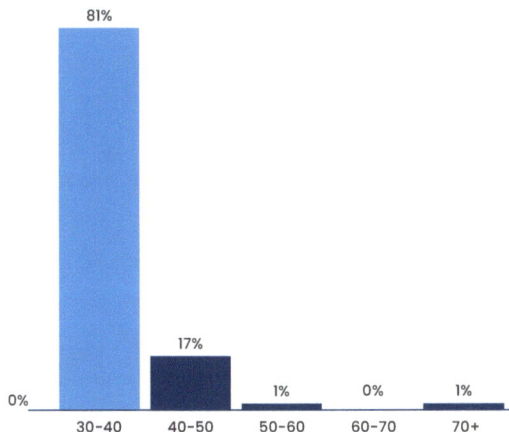

- 30–40: 81%
- 40–50: 17%
- 50–60: 1%
- 60–70: 0%
- 70+: 1%

Would I enjoy the work?

- ☺ Supportive, inclusive work culture
- ☺ Broad scope of work available
- ☺ Supportive colleagues and mentors
- ☹ Outdated software systems
- ☹ Limited opportunities for technical development
- ☹ Lack of career progression and certainty

Average rating
4.1
out of
5.0
★★★★☆

On the job

Jake Keenan

Bachelor of Commerce
(Finance) and Science
(Mathematics and Statistics),
Master of Data Science;
University of New South Wales

Data Graduate at Australian
Taxation Office (ATO)

Australian Government
Australian Taxation Office

'The ATO is
modernising its
existing architecture,
moving to a cloud-
based solution,
and it's my job to
leverage these
services to identify
fraud using data
science.'

What's your job about?

The ATO is modernising its existing architecture, moving to a cloud-based solution, and it's my job to leverage these services to identify fraud using data science. In my current rotation as a Data Graduate, I'm currently using Python and Structured Query Language (SQL) to analyse fraudulent patterns in various datasets. This process involves applying data cleaning, wrangling, and visualisation techniques to gain better insights into the data.

What's your background?

During my time at school, I was always unsure about the career path I wanted to pursue. It wasn't until I reached year 11 that I came across a real passion for Mathematics, thanks to my teacher. I ended up sticking to and graduating with a Bachelor of Commerce (Finance) and Bachelor of Science (Maths & Stats). During this period, I also worked as a Customer Service Representative at a local supermarket.

After working at a few jobs, I knew I wanted to go back to university to undertake further study. However, it wasn't until Covid struck that I enrolled back at UNSW to pursue a Master of Data Science. I successfully graduated, achieving my long-desired goal! I applied for a position as an ATO Data Graduate and was so pleased when I found out my application was successful.

Could someone with a different background do your job?

If you come from a business background, then you would have an understanding of how to interpret data, which is vital. However, you would need to have experience in programming languages such as Python and SQL as well as skills in maths, such as machine learning and statistical modelling. But there are many courses that can teach you these skills, which are easily accessible online or by attending university.

What's the coolest thing about your job?

One is the flexibility the ATO provides in terms of when you start and finish. For many people, the standard 9-5 doesn't work, so having that extra flexibility to adjust your start time is great.

Secondly, you really get noticed for the hard work you do. For example, during my first rotation, I created an automated solution to solve an existing business problem, and it certainly didn't go unnoticed. I got to present my idea to our Senior Executive, who was in charge of the broader team I was placed in, which was an awesome experience.

What are the limitations of your job?

I think the worst limitation of the job is its rotation based. Basically, you complete approximately two six-month rotations with a contact centre experience in between but that does give you some good experiences. If you're a person that prefers alternating between different teams and learning how they function, operate, and work, this job is ideal, and I'd highly encourage you to apply.

On the job

Namita Jose

Bachelor of Systems
Engineering; Australian
National University

Air Vehicle Systems Engineer
at Department of Defence

'It's pretty exciting
coming to work
and to bring each
of the RAAF's fifth-
generation fighter
aircraft into service.
The F-35A features
a range of cutting-
edge technologies. It
is a rare opportunity
and it's something
that, as an engineer,
you don't get to
experience that
often.'

How did you get to your current job position?

I started off studying a Bachelor of Veterinary Biology/Doctor of Veterinary Medicine at the University of Sydney but after two years decided this wasn't for me and transferred to a Bachelor of Science majoring in Biology. Afterwards, I was immediately attracted to jobs in the public sector and discovered the NSW Government Graduate Program and applied. I started in the Program in February 2019 at the Department of Planning, Industry and Environment (DPIE).

What does your employer do?

My team at DPIE is working on developing the Cumberland Plain Conservation Plan (CPCP) for the bio-certification of growth areas in Western Sydney. This involves strategically planning the location and management of conservation sites which offset the damage caused by development in growth areas.

What are your areas of responsibility?

My main responsibilities include helping create, edit and update the Monitoring, Evaluation and Reporting framework for the CPCP, and helping manage the team's relationships with our stakeholders and delivery partners. I acted as the single point of contact between the branch and a consultancy firm and acted as secretariat at a weekly meeting with them. I conducted a lot of research projects, such as the potential use of blockchain technology for our project and possible survey methods for the different threatened species in our project area.

What are the career prospects with your job?

After we successfully complete the Graduate Program, we are offered a permanent role in our home agency. The skills I have learnt so far in the Program will be applicable to many different roles.

What do you love the most about your job?

I love that my job allows me to make a difference in the lives of the people of NSW and the environment in NSW. I love that my job allows me to have a good work-life balance, mentoring, networking, training and skill development. I also love that I am exposed to a wide variety of different tasks and my managers have both really tried to help me develop my skills in my areas of interest.

What's the biggest limitation of your job?

Having three six-month rotations is good for access to a variety of tasks and workplaces – it can feel a little difficult moving as you feel as though you are just getting the hang of everything before you are moved to another place, but this does not detract from the Program. In the way of stress, I bear a level of responsibility suitable for me and if I ever need help with anything, I am always able to get support from my team.

Law

Photo courtesy of Clyde & Co.

Law is all about helping others with their legal needs. These could be individuals, businesses, the government – heck, wherever people and organisations need help with rules, agreements, and their rights, you'll find lawyers.

Private sector law

This is law in the business world, which means you'd handle business contracts, corporate law, intellectual property, and more. There are two main paths in the private sector:

- **Private practice:** You can work at a law firm, offering various services to people and businesses, specialising in a specific area, and often representing clients in court or negotiations.

- **In-house:** Alternatively, you could work as in-house legal counsel at a company, handling all their legal matters, from contracts to compliance.

Public service and public interest law

This is law in the world of government and not-for-profits.

- **Government & public service:** You might find yourself working for the government - be it local, state, or national - where you'll help guide the government's decisions with your legal expertise.

- **Judicial system:** Or you could work within the court system. Here, you might be arguing cases as a prosecutor or even making decisions as a judge.

- **Public interest law & social justice:** This is all about using your skills to advocate for important causes like civil rights, economic equality, environmental protection, consumer safety - issues that really shape society.

Where are the best places to work?

Here are recent grads' top picks for working in the legal field:

Sector Rank	Employer	Location of opportunities	Accepting applications from / Types of opportunities	Learn more
#1	**Herbert Smith Freehills** **4.4** ★★★★½ **#40 Overall**	📍 Brisbane, Melbourne, Perth, Sydney	**L** Graduate jobs Clerkships	Page 153
#2	**Ashurst** **4.4** ★★★★½ **#47 Overall**	📍 Sydney, Melbourne, Brisbane, Canberra, Perth	**L** Graduate jobs Clerkships	Page 157
#3	**Allens** **4.5** ★★★★½ **#75 Overall**	📍 Sydney, Melbourne, Brisbane, Perth	**L** Graduate jobs Clerkships	Page 171
#4	**Clayton Utz** **3.8** ★★★★☆ **#96 Overall**	📍 Sydney, Melbourne, Brisbane, Perth, Canberra	**L** Graduate jobs Clerkships	Page 181
#5	**MinterEllison** **4.3** ★★★★☆ **#99 Overall**	📍 Sydney, Melbourne, Canberra, Darwin, Perth, Brisbane, Adelaide, work from home	**B C E H I** **L M P S T** Graduate jobs Clerkships	Page 183

The firms that made our ranking are mostly 'Big Law' firms, which usually serve major corporations and are characterised by their extensive global or regional presence.

They're definitely a great place to launch your legal career, but if the stress and long hours don't appeal to you, you can also find plenty of graduate law programs at companies and government agencies on our top 100 list.

What jobs are there?

Graduate law roles

Graduate law programs are designed to equip you with a strong foundation in legal practice through hands-on work and comprehensive training.

You'll be trained not only on legal skills but also other aspects necessary for a successful legal career – think: negotiation, client communication, and business development.

You'll get to rotate across different departments to sample the different kinds of legal work, helping you decide what you're best suited for.

You'll also have opportunities for mentorship, professional development, and networking, all while working alongside experienced lawyers.

Some firms may even offer global secondment opportunities where graduates can work in an overseas office for a period of time!

Tip: If you're interested in working at a law firm, don't wait until your final year to apply! Apply for a clerkship or internship during your second or third year. Law firms often hire graduates who have previously interned with them, so starting early improves your chances.

Legal operations roles

At the end of the day, law firms are businesses and they need people to keep the business side of things running smoothly so lawyers can focus on practising the law. This is where legal operations come in.

Legal operations professionals take care of things like budgeting and project management.

Legal analyst roles

A legal analyst is a professional who helps lawyers and legal teams by conducting research, organising information, and preparing legal documents.

By handling tasks such as document drafting and research, legal analysts free up attorneys to focus more on the strategic aspects of legal work, client relationships, and court appearances.

Corporate support

In recent years, the top law firms have hired HR and Learning & Development graduates.

Tech & data roles

Top law firms are increasingly relying on technology and data to stay competitive. This has given rise to graduate programs in these fields.

In a tech or data role, you might build systems and databases or stay on top of developments in legal technology to incorporate into the firm's practice.

Roles at top companies in order of salary

Here are the jobs that the top-ranked companies have posted on our site and how much they pay.

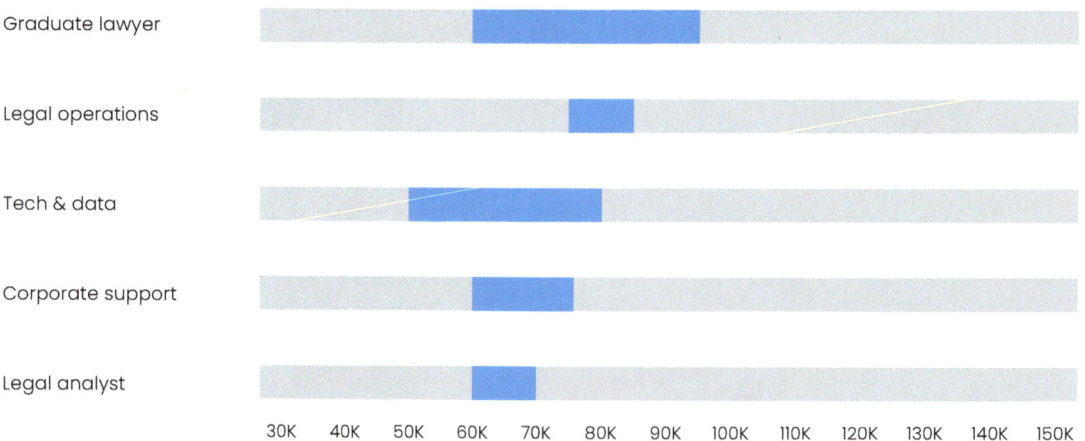

Graduate lawyer	60K–95K
Legal operations	75K–85K
Tech & data	50K–80K
Corporate support	60K–70K
Legal analyst	60K–70K

Scale: 30K 40K 50K 60K 70K 80K 90K 100K 110K 120K 130K 140K 150K

Is it for me?

Do I need a relevant degree?

91%
of recent grads
in this sector studied
Law, legal studies & justice

| Humanities, arts & social sciences | 5% |
| Other | 4% |

How much would I work each week?

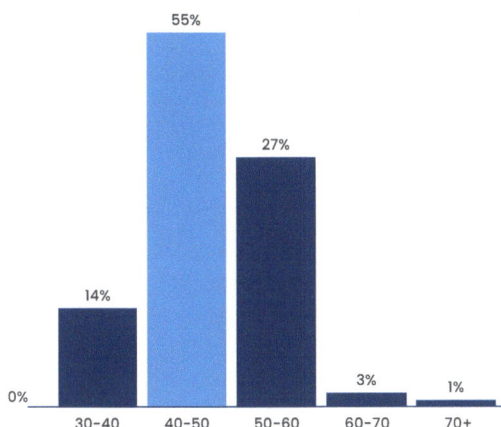

- 30-40: 14%
- 40-50: 55%
- 50-60: 27%
- 60-70: 3%
- 70+: 1%
- 0%

How much would I make?

Average pay by region

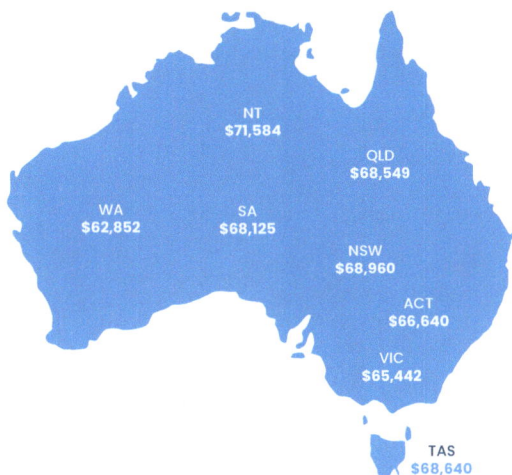

- NT $71,584
- QLD $68,549
- WA $62,852
- SA $68,125
- NSW $68,960
- ACT $66,640
- VIC $65,442
- TAS $68,640

Average salary
$64-$73K

Average hourly wage
$27.91

Would I enjoy the work?

- ☺ Working with talented and intelligent colleagues
- ☺ Engaging in interesting and challenging work
- ☺ Ability to work on international matters or participate in overseas secondments
- ☹ Hierarchical structures and lack of opportunities for learning and growth, particularly for junior employees
- ☹ Inadequate compensation for the hours worked
- ☹ Lack of transparency around pay and career progression

Average rating

4.3
out of
5.0

★★★★½

On the job

Tayla Byatt

Juris Doctor & Bachelor of
Commerce; University of
Western Australia

Graduate, Perth
at Herbert Smith Freehills

HERBERT
SMITH
FREEHILLS

'I was lucky to work
on some really
interesting tasks
during my clerkship.
This included doing
some work for
Natasha Blycha
on the Australian
National Blockchain
project, and drafting
research notes
on various topics,
such as the GDPR
and 'Right to be
Forgotten'. I also
helped draft a
contract for a race
car event.'

Scan to
read more
graduate stories

Tell us about yourself?

My name is Tayla Byatt, and I am starting as a graduate at the
Perth HSF office. I completed the Juris Doctor at UWA and also hold
a Bachelor of Commerce. I completed my vacation clerkship in
the Technology, Media and Telecommunication Team. I was also a
paralegal in the Real Estate team for 10 months.

What was your pathway to HSF?

The first memory I have of HSF was a seminar organised by the
Law Faculty Club, where they put together a skit on 'interview
tips'. The skit was hilarious and engaging as the grad who was
the 'bad example' walked in 20 minutes late, talked back to the
partner and started texting during the interview, all while sporting
a fluoro wind breaker jacket. It was nice to see a firm that could
have some fun and seemed to all get along. When clerkship
applications came around, I was intrigued to find out more about
the firm and their culture. During my interview, we spent most of
the time talking about my family chicken farm and our favourite
movies – it honestly didn't feel like an interview at all. From this,
I was not only lucky enough to be offered a clerkship, but also a
paralegal position. During both roles, I loved the variety of work, the
opportunities available, and the fact everyone treated each other
like family. Whether it be the tailored birthday emails from Pam (the
team's Legal Secretary) or the way the firm kept in touch even when
I was not working and overseas on exchange.

**What were your expectations before joining HSF? How did your
experience match or differ from your expectations?**

Being the first in my family to go into law, most of my expectations
prior to clerkships and starting law school came from TV shows
like Suits and The Good Wife. The classic junior solicitors are hidden
away in cubicles away from the partners, not being allowed to talk
to them or ignored. At HSF, this could not be further from the truth,
as no matter your role, you always sit with your team, allowing you
to listen and observe everyone completing their day-to-day tasks,
and constantly receiving advice and feedback. I was also able to
work directly with the partners of the firm on numerous occasions,
and never felt like I couldn't approach them with questions.

**The most interesting/surprising thing you've learned – either
about law, yourself, or HSF – during your time here?**

I think the fact that everyone's legal career was different. There were
lawyers with backgrounds in physics, engineering and data science,
those who have moved into entrepreneurial roles and working on
technology to move the firm forward. There was also a range of
working arrangements, allowing people to work across different

offices and from home (even before COVID). It was interesting to see how each person was able to shape their legal career to reflect who they were and what they want to achieve.

Can you think of a time when you had a meaningful impact at work?

I was lucky to work on some really interesting tasks during my clerkship. This included doing some work for Natasha Blycha on the Australian National Blockchain project, and drafting research notes on various topics, such as the GDPR and 'Right to be Forgotten'. I also helped draft a contract for a race car event.

What piece of advice would you give someone considering a role at HSF?

Make the time to reach out and talk to a variety of people from the firm, and from different practice groups (even the ones you don't think you're interested in). Everyone has had a different journey, and can provide their own perspectives as they are all willing to make some time to speak to you and pass on advice to help you make decisions about your own career.

How has your experience, background & skills outside of your legal skills, helped you contribute as a grad/clerk?

It's a bit niche, but the fact I grew up on a chicken farm and continued to work there throughout my degree, always acted as a really good conversation starter when meeting clients or anyone else at HSF.

Management consulting

Just as we all sometimes need a little good advice, so do businesses. That's where consulting comes into play - it's all about offering expert guidance to businesses when they need it most.

But what does management consulting mean? Is it advice for managers? Not exactly.

- Management here doesn't refer to your run-of-the-mill middle manager.

- Instead, it refers to the work of managing a business – i.e. its resources, processes, technologies, and people – to help it succeed.

- It's about making big-picture decisions and steering the direction of the entire company.

So management consulting firms are in the business of helping businesses make important decisions! They do this by:

- **Conducting research and analysis** into a business's markets, their competition, and their operations.

- **Developing strategies,** which can range from expanding into new markets to restructuring the organisation.

- **Implementing changes** – at some firms, consultants also guide the firm in carrying out their recommendations.

Where are the best places to work?

Sector Rank	Employer	Location of opportunities	Accepting applications from / Types of opportunities	Learn more
#1	**Capgemini Australia and New Zealand** `4.8` ★★★★★ #1 Overall	Sydney, Melbourne, Brisbane, Adelaide, Hobart, Canberra, Auckland, Wellington, Christchurch	B C E H I L M P S T Graduate jobs Internships	Page 134
#2	**Oliver Wyman Australia & New Zealand** `4.0` ★★★★☆ #8 Overall	Melbourne, Perth, Sydney	B C E H I L M P S T Graduate jobs Internships	Page 137
#3	**Kearney** `4.2` ★★★★☆ #19 Overall	Sydney, Melbourne	B C E H I L M P S T Graduate jobs Internships	Page 143
#4	**Nous Group** `4.3` ★★★★☆ #21 Overall	Melbourne, Sydney, Canberra, Brisbane, Perth, Darwin	B C E H I L M P S T Graduate jobs Internships	Page 144
#5	**Accenture Australia and New Zealand** `3.8` ★★★★☆ #32 Overall	Sydney, Melbourne, Brisbane, Perth, Adelaide, Canberra, Auckland, Wellington	B C E H I L M P S T Graduate jobs Internships	Page 149

What jobs are there?

Business consulting roles

This category includes entry-level strategy and management consulting roles, which involves doing research and analysis, and making presentations.

You'll get to undergo rigorous training to learn all the tools and frameworks you need to analyse businesses and provide actionable insights.

Tech & data consulting roles

On the tech side of things, you'd do things like introduce clients to new software tools and suggest ways for them to manage their cybersecurity risks.

On the data side of things, you'd help companies make sense of their data so they can better understand their customers, spot trends, or run more efficiently.

IT & tech roles

These are technical roles like 'software engineer' or 'application support engineer' which would have you developing and maintaining software for clients.

Corporate support

In recent years, consulting firms have hired a limited number of corporate support roles in HR and finance.

Roles at top companies in order of salary

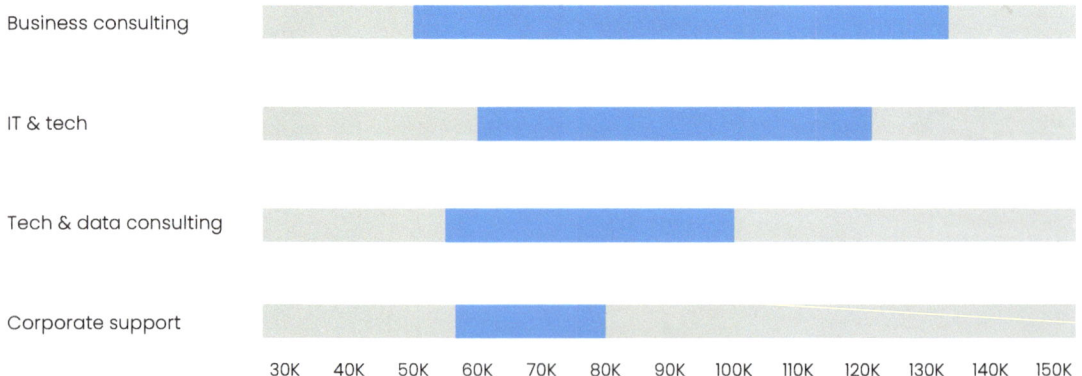

Business consulting	~50K – ~130K
IT & tech	~55K – ~120K
Tech & data consulting	~55K – ~100K
Corporate support	~55K – ~80K

30K 40K 50K 60K 70K 80K 90K 100K 110K 120K 130K 140K 150K

Is it for me?

Do I need a relevant degree?

33%
of recent grads
in this sector studied
IT & computer science

Business & management	24%
Engineering & mathematics	18%
Humanities, arts & social sciences	7%
Sciences	7%
Finance, accounting, economics & business administration	5%
Other	6%

How much would I make?

Average pay by region

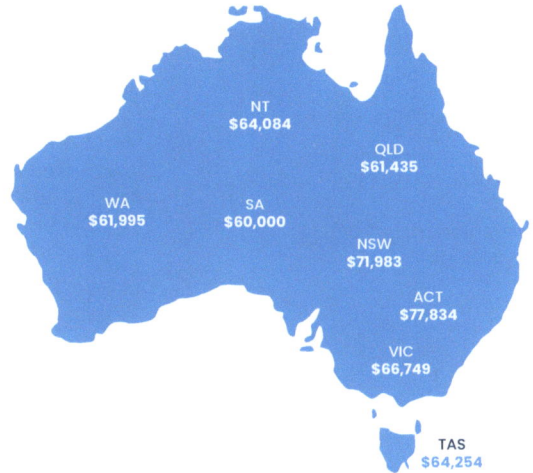

NT $64,084

QLD $61,435

WA $61,995

SA $60,000

NSW $71,983

ACT $77,834

VIC $66,749

TAS $64,254

Average salary
$62–$72K

Average hourly wage
$26.42

How much would I work each week?

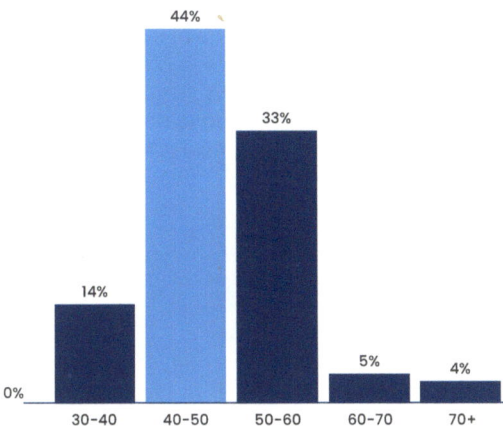

- 30–40: 14%
- 40–50: 44%
- 50–60: 33%
- 60–70: 5%
- 70+: 4%
- (0%)

Would I enjoy the work?

- ☺ Flexible working arrangements
- ☺ Working with colleagues of different levels of experience, cultures, and ideals
- ☺ Supportive and collaborative environment
- ☹ High turnover
- ☹ Mundane or repetitive work
- ☹ Being placed on projects that may not align with one's interests or skills

Average rating

4.2 out of 5.0

★★★★☆

On the job

Joseph Nguyen

Bachelor of Commerce;
Curtin University

Senior Consultant
at Nous Group

nous

'I do really love having the opportunity to work on a range of projects that actually make a difference. For instance, last year I engaged with an Aboriginal community in regional WA to inform their new Housing Strategy (including with Elders on their traditional land), which I found particularly cool and don't think I'd be able to do in many other jobs.'

What's your job about?

Nous is a management consulting firm. I still have trouble explaining what this is to friends and family – but essentially, organisations (public, private or not-for-profit) generally look to engage Nous when they have a problem but don't have the capacity or capability to solve it internally. Most of the work we do is in the public sector.

As a consultant on projects, my role is typically to help structure and write deliverables. These are often in the form of a report that outlines the key findings and recommendations we have developed to a client's problem. We typically inform these deliverables in two ways:

1. Conducting stakeholder engagements
2. Undertaking desktop research

Therefore, my day-to-day tasks often involve conducting research, creating materials for stakeholder engagements (e.g. PowerPoint slides to present, and interview guides) and writing reports (typically in Microsoft Word or PowerPoint).

What's your background?

I was born and raised in Perth, WA. I realised mid-way through high school that I hated even trying to turn on a Bunsen Burner, concluded that I didn't think a career in science would be for me and found that I quite liked Economics – so thought I'd pursue a career in business and went all in on business-related subjects (Accounting, Economics, Business Management). I'm not sure I would recommend this approach to everyone as I still see the value in keeping options open, and sometimes wish I continued with Chemistry to see if I'd like it further (but alas here we are!).

My business-minded ATAR subjects naturally led me to pursue a commerce degree, and I decided to do this at Curtin University in Perth. My first year took me a bit of adjusting – I was quite lazy and didn't get involved. I took a leap of faith and applied to a university consulting club in my second year. I really enjoyed it, but wasn't 100% sure if I was all in on consulting.

I completed a few internships in different areas such as accounting, finance and international business. I applied for a grad job at Nous as I still wasn't really sure what exactly I wanted to do, so the idea of working on a ton of different projects I found exciting. Fortunately, I got the job and have been here for around 1.5 years.

Scan to
read more
graduate stories

Could someone with a different background do your job?

Definitely. There is such a diverse range of degrees at Nous (Commerce, Arts, Health/Science, etc.). Nous largely looks at your ability to think in a structured way, draw out key findings from data (qualitative and quantitative), and communicate insights in a clear and compelling way for clients (usually through PowerPoint or Word). You will be dealing with a lot of people on the job, including clients and colleagues, so the ability to engage with different people is also important.

A lot of these things you will learn by doing, so I'd say a keen attitude and willingness to learn are the keys!

What's the coolest thing about your job?

I do really love having the opportunity to work on a range of projects that actually make a difference. For instance, last year I engaged with an Aboriginal community in regional WA to inform their new Housing Strategy (including with Elders on their traditional land), which I found particularly cool and don't think I'd be able to do in many other jobs.

What are the limitations of your job?

Delivering to client deadlines and working across multiple projects means you can sometimes be working late nights and weekends. This can be mentally tiring and it can be hard to 'switch off', especially if you consistently have a heavy workload. Luckily, Nous's self-management model promotes taking 'recharge leave' if you feel you've had a period of really high intensity and need time off.

3 pieces of advice for yourself when you were a student...

- Take your time! There is really no rush to get into a career and get to the top – most of us will be working for 30-40 years when you think about it so what's the rush?

- 'Lean in' and try out different things – I only learnt about consulting because I took a leap of faith and interviewed for a consulting club at uni. I also regret not going on a Semester Abroad, which got taken away partly due to COVID. It's unlikely there is a period in your life that you have as much free time as a university (although it doesn't feel like it), so if you can, try out as many different opportunities as possible.

- Mingle and meet new people – as a natural introvert I know this one can be particularly tough, but this is a great time to socialise and try and make new friends as everyone is really discovering themselves and their passions.

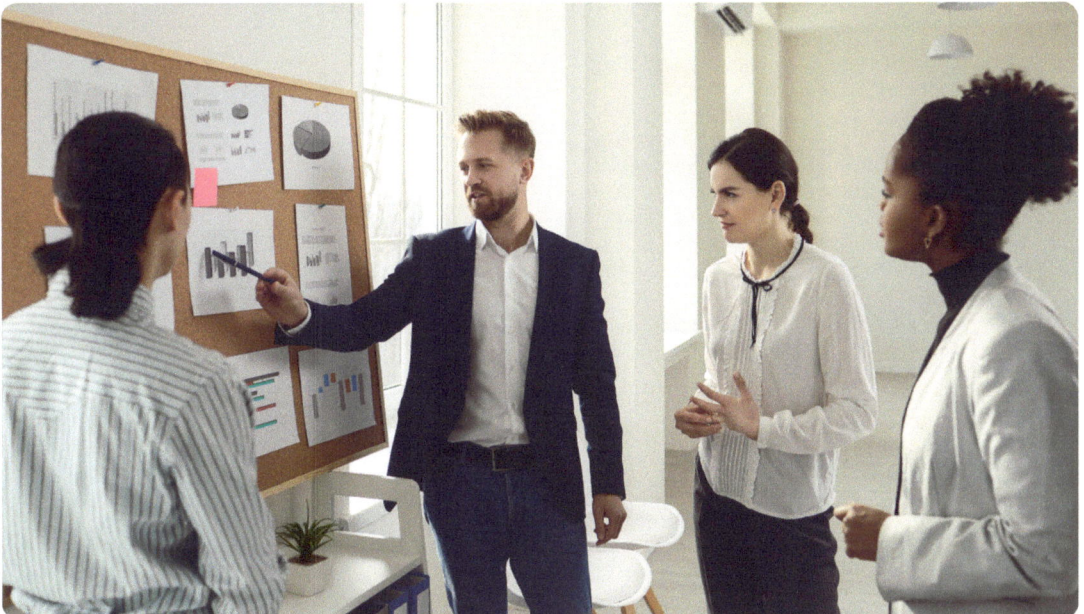

Mining, energy, oil & gas

Note: 'Mining, energy, oil & gas' is broken into two distinct sectors on our website: 'Mining, Oil & Gas' and 'Energy & Utilities.'

Mining, oil & gas

The mining, oil & gas sector is all about extracting valuable natural resources from the Earth.

- With mining, we're digging up metals like gold, silver, iron, and copper, as well as non-metals like coal and diamonds. Mining is important because these materials are used in everything from our jewellery and coins to our cars, houses, and electronic devices.

- In the case of oil & gas, we're getting valuable resources in liquid or gas form. We use oil and gas for a ton of things in our lives, from fueling our cars and heating our homes to making plastics and other materials.

Energy & utilities

The energy & utilities sector is responsible for:

- **Generating electricity** with coal, gas, hydro, and wind power stations.

- **Delivering electricity and other utilities** (like water and natural gas) to our homes, schools, offices … wherever it's needed!

- **Selling electricity and other utilities to consumers.**

- **Handling waste disposal and treatment** – think: trash collection, recycling, and sewage treatment.

Here's what top companies in this space do.

- The oil and gas producers tend to be major players worldwide. The biggest ones are integrated energy companies, which means they take care of the full range of operations from exploration and production to refining and distribution.

- There are also companies that just focus on mining as well as companies that operate across the whole spectrum of mining, oil, and natural gas.

- Finally, there are also some utilities companies that are responsible for distributing electrical power around the country.

Where are the best places to work?

Sector Rank	Employer	Location of opportunities	Accepting applications from / Types of opportunities	Learn more
Mining, oil & gas				
#1	**BHP** **4.2** ★★★★☆ #17 Overall	⦿ Queensland, South Australia, Western Australia	B E H I L M P S T **Graduate jobs** **Internships**	Page 142
#2	**Rio Tinto** **4.0** ★★★★☆ #44 Overall	⦿ Multiple locations in Australia and New Zealand	B E H I P P S **Graduate jobs** **Internships**	Page 155
#3	**Woodside Energy** **3.9** ★★★★☆ #46 Overall	⦿ Perth, with some site based rotational opportunities available in Karratha	B C E H I L M P S T **Graduate jobs** **Internships**	Page 156
Energy & utilities				
#1	**Transgrid** **4.3** ★★★★☆ #76 Overall	⦿ New South Wales	B C E H I L M P S T **Graduate jobs** **Internships**	Page 171
#2	**Australian Energy Market Operator (AEMO)** **4.4** ★★★★☆ #80 Overall	⦿ Melbourne, Sydney, Norwest, Brisbane, Perth, Adelaide	B E I S **Graduate jobs** **Internships**	Page 173

What jobs are there?

Engineering & geosciences roles

The largest number of roles at mining companies are in engineering.

Chemical and mechanical engineering graduates will get hands-on experience dealing with the machines and power systems that are needed to mine.

If you have a background in civil engineering, environmental engineering, geology, or geotechnics, you can qualify for a mining engineer role, where you would help figure out how to extract minerals out of the ground in the safest and most efficient way).

You'll also find roles in petroleum engineering, materials engineering, and process engineering.

Tech & data roles

As the industry is becoming more digitalised, mining, energy, oil & gas companies have hired more and more employees focused on tech & data.

You might use your technical background to help safeguard a company's computer systems or analyse data to improve safety, sustainability, and productivity.

Safety & sustainability roles

Finally, there's a small number of safety & sustainability roles.

These roles are about keeping people and the environment safe. You'd help make sure workers and nearby communities stay healthy, keep the work environment safe and secure, and work hard to limit any negative effects on the environment.

Roles at top companies in order of salary

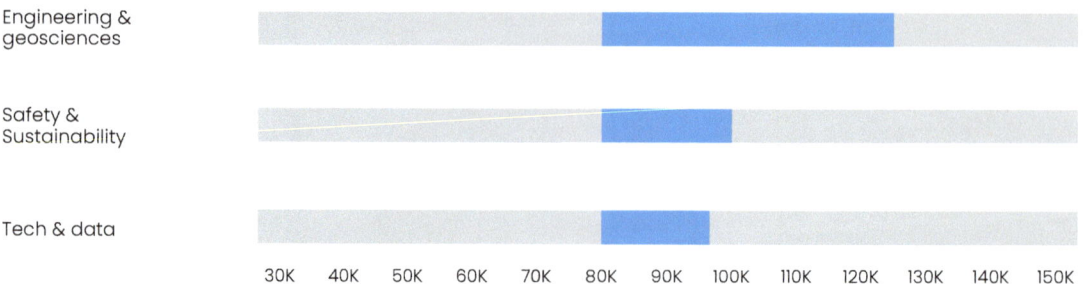

	30K	40K	50K	60K	70K	80K	90K	100K	110K	120K	130K	140K	150K
Engineering & geosciences													
Safety & Sustainability													
Tech & data													

Is it for me?

Do I need a relevant degree?

Mining, oil & gas

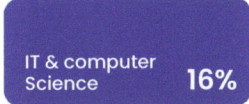

57%
of recent grads
in this sector studied
**Engineering &
mathematics**

IT & computer Science	**16%**
Sciences	**14%**
Other	**13%**

Energy & utilities

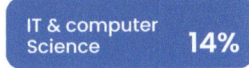

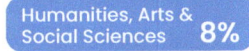

62%
of recent grads
in this sector studied
**Engineering &
mathematics**

IT & computer Science	**14%**
Humanities, Arts & Social Sciences	**8%**
Business & management	**7%**
Sciences	**4%**
Other	**4%**

How much would I make?

Average pay by region

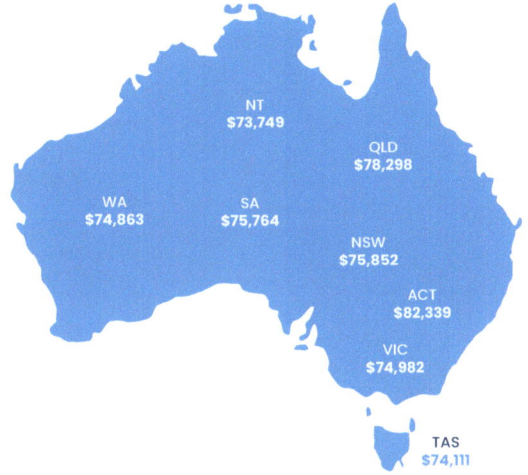

NT $73,749
QLD $78,298
WA $74,863
SA $75,764
NSW $75,852
ACT $82,339
VIC $74,982
TAS $74,111

Mining, oil & gas
$77–$92K
Average salary

$33.89
Average hourly wage

Energy & utilities
$70–$90K
Average salary

$37.14
Average hourly wage

How much would I work each week?

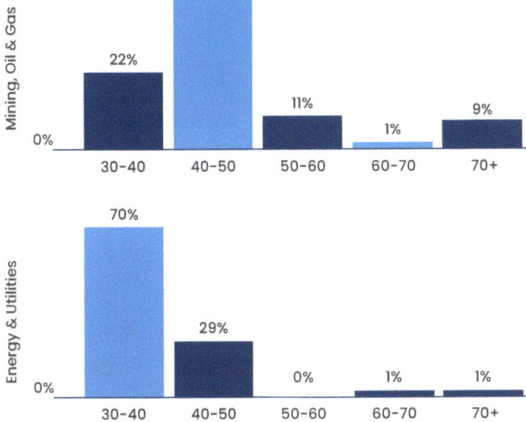

Mining, Oil & Gas

30–40	40–50	50–60	60–70	70+
22%	57%	11%	1%	9%

Energy & Utilities

30–40	40–50	50–60	60–70	70+
70%	29%	0%	1%	1%

Would I enjoy the work?

Mining, oil & gas
- ☺ Flexibility in working hours
- ☺ Exposure to a variety of projects and challenges
- ☺ Good salary and benefits
- ☹ Lack of on-the-job training
- ☹ Frequent travel for work
- ☹ Inconsistent work assignments

Energy & utilities
- ☺ Meaningful and rewarding work that contributes positively to the community
- ☺ Supportive colleagues and positive work culture
- ☺ Flexible work arrangements including flexible hours and work from home options
- ☹ Bureaucracy
- ☹ Lack of communication between teams
- ☹ Limited opportunities for site visits or field work

4.2 OUT OF 5.0 Average rating ★★★★☆

On the job

Nisha Nijhar

Bachelor of Science in Mechanical Engineering & Master of Engineering, Mechanical Engineering with Business; University of Melbourne

Mining Equipment Maintenance (MEM) Reliability Engineer at BHP

BHP

'My role's purpose is to execute defect elimination processes, provide specialist advice and undertake reliability improvement focused on the end-to-end maintenance system (inclusive of procedures, work quality, processes, and materials) – specifically for the ancillary mining equipment; these are the loaders, graders and dozers used by our Mining teams.'

Scan to read more **graduate stories**

5:01 AM

It's a Monday! Up and ready to fly in to work today.

I am on a 5/2/4/3 FIFO (Fly-In-Fly-Out) roster – which goes five days on shift (Monday to Friday), two days off shift (Saturday and Sunday), four days on shift (Monday to Thursday), three days off shift (Friday to Sunday), and repeat; in short, I am back home in Perth every weekend and every second Friday which is great!

I always say goodbye to my sleepy dogs before heading to the airport.

5:24 AM

I am a fan of watching the sunrise on my way to the airport.

My work days are 12 hours long – 6.00 am to 6.00 pm; my flight times are accounted for on the days I fly in and out at BHP, which is great! Today my flight departs Perth at 6.20 am and arrives at Newman at 8.05 am – I will be enjoying a plane nap during this time.

8:14 AM

Arrived in sunny Newman and straight onto the bus with everyone else – I enjoyed listening to podcasts during this commute. We will be stopping by one of the Villages (these are FIFO accommodation sites in/around Newman town) to pack our food for the day, then off to site!

8:31 AM

Crib pitstop. I usually pack the following for a day at work:

Sandwich for breakfast (today it was a Tomato and Mozzarella Salad Roll)

Main meal of some kind for lunch (today it was Cauliflower Curry and Rice).

Two pieces of fruit to snack on (today it was a Green Apple and a Mandarin).

Another sandwich (today it was a Ham and Cheese Toastie) and a salad for an early dinner (today it was a Garden Salad with added Cherry Tomatoes)

9:15 AM

Made it to the office. Time to check my emails – I try to keep my number of unread emails at zero by the end of each work week.

In my Mining Equipment Maintenance Reliability team, I am currently the Reliability Engineer for all Ancillary Equipment across Newman Operations (this covers both BHP's Newman West and Newman East mine sites). My role's purpose is to execute defect elimination processes, provide specialist advice and undertake reliability improvement focused on the end-to-end maintenance system) – specifically for the ancillary mining equipment; these are the loaders, graders and dozers used by our Mining teams.

One of my core routines to contribute toward me executing my role effectively is reviewing data from the previous week to put a Weekly Report together every Monday. After I sift through my emails, and put my Weekly Report together, I decide which key areas to focus my attention on for the week and onwards. The Weekly Report gets sent to my MEM Ancillary Execution teams – these are the teams who carry out the maintenance required on the machines I am interested in improving reliability of. They know the machines well and I rely on their expertise and knowledge to assist in maintaining reliability of the machines.

1:12 PM

After lunch, I venture out toward the Mining Equipment Workshop (MEW), which is a 5–10-minute walk from my office building, depending on how quickly I opt to move. It is top of 42 degrees (Celsius) in Newman today – Summer is well and truly upon us. I always bring my wide brim hat and water bottle with me when heading outside.

1:18 PM

Looks like a busy day in the MEW with all bays occupied. We have a line-up of track dozers and we also have a grader in the image below, with a dump truck getting a shower in the background.

I like to spend as much time as I can in the MEW with the Execution team to check in on how the machines are doing and take on any feedback which they have for me at the time – especially if there are any early warning signs which I can investigate further to ensure we have appropriate controls put in place to avoid any unplanned breakdowns.

I also take this time in the workshop with Execution to ask questions and learn more about the machines, to improve my knowledge of them, which assists me in carrying out my job more effectively.

5:58 PM

After some more desk work and a meeting back in my office building, my work for the day is done!

6:29 PM

Caught sight of a faint rainbow in the distance as a light shower came through on my way to the gym for a yoga class, as seen in the image below – I always look forward to this class which runs between 6.30 pm and 7.30 pm on Mondays; it is a great way to start the week for me.

8:30 PM

After a shower and short video chat with my partner, I am in bed and ready for a good night's rest to do it all again tomorrow.

Retail & consumer goods

Photo courtesy of the Kraft Heinz Company

The retail & consumer goods sector is made up of companies that make and sell things that we buy for our own use and enjoyment – everything from our clothes to our TV.

Consumer goods

Let's start with consumer goods. Companies in this category are focused on making and marketing products to attract consumers. Their products can be divided into two main types: 'durable' and 'non-durable.'

- **Durable goods** are items that stick with us for the long haul - think three years or more. They're that shiny new car, hardworking appliance, comfy furniture, or high-tech gadget that we spend a good amount of money on as an investment into our future comfort and convenience.

- **Non-durable goods** tend to be cheaper items like food, clothing, and personal care products that we use up within a year or less.

Retail

If consumer goods companies are about making products, retail companies are focused on selling products.

Some consumer goods companies also sell their own creations – Apple and Nike are prime examples. For the most part though, consumer

goods companies leave the selling to retail businesses … which is understandable, considering how much work it is. Just take a look at all the things retailers take care of:

- **Sales & customer service:** This involves helping customers find what they need, providing product information, handling transactions, and assisting with returns or exchanges.

- **Inventory management:** Retailers manage their stock levels to ensure they have enough products to meet customer demand without overstocking.

- **Merchandising:** This involves displaying products in a way that encourages customers to make purchases. It can include window displays, in-store layouts, and promotional displays.

- **Advertising & promotions:** Retailers use advertising, sales promotions, social media campaigns, and loyalty programs to attract and retain customers.

- **After-sales services:** Think product warranties, repairs, and maintenance.

And that's not all! On top of this, many retailers now provide e-commerce services, which involves running an online store, handling online orders and returns, and providing customer service through email, live chat, and social media.

Where are the best places to work?

Sector Rank	Employer		Location of opportunities	Accepting applications from / Types of opportunities	Learn more
#1	L'ORÉAL	**L'Oréal Australia & New Zealand** 4.2 ★★★★☆ #14 Overall	⊙ Melbourne, Auckland	B C E H I L M P S T Graduate jobs Internships	Page 140
#2	coles group	**Coles** 4.2 ★★★★☆ #20 Overall	⊙ Victoria	B C E H I L M P S T Graduate jobs	Page 143
#3	Unilever	**Unilever Australia and New Zealand** 4.3 ★★★★☆ #55 Overall	⊙ Sydney, Auckland	B C E H I L M P S T Graduate jobs Internships	Page 161
#4	DuluxGroup	**Dulux Group** 4.3 ★★★★☆ #67 Overall	⊙ New South Wales, Queensland, Victoria, South Australia, Western Australia	B C E H I L M P S T Graduate jobs	Page 167
#5	Kraft Heinz	**Kraft Heinz Company** 4.2 ★★★★☆ #70 Overall	⊙ Melbourne, Seven Hills, Northgate	B C E H I L S Graduate jobs	Page 168

These companies fall into two main categories.

- **Fast-moving consumer goods (FMCG):** FMCG companies make non-durable goods that sell quickly and often cheaply. FMCGs account for a significant portion of sales in this sector and offer a fast-paced and exciting environment to launch your career.

- **Retail:** Retail may not sound like an exciting sector to launch your career, but it's actually full of opportunities to learn, grow, and make an impact – whether you're creating exceptional customer experiences or shaping the way we live, eat, and dress.

What jobs are there?

Business & commercial graduate roles

In a business graduate program, you would get to work across various business units, functions, and locations, gaining a holistic understanding of the company.

Keep an eye out for management trainee programs, which are designed to groom future leaders of the company.

Supply chain & operations roles

Supply chain management is about planning what products to make, buying the materials to make them, creating the products, packaging them, getting them to stores, and making sure the products are always available when customers want to buy them.

Because the supply chain is so important to retail & consumer goods companies, they tend to have graduate programs focused specifically on this aspect of their operations.

In these programs, you'll get real-world experience handling supply chain management and, depending on the company, exposure to other key operations as well.

Tech & data roles

Retail & consumer goods companies need to nurture their own tech talent so they can stay ahead in this increasingly digital world. That's why some companies in this space have started having tech & data-focused graduate programs.

In these programs, you'll get to apply your technical skills to practical situations, like developing software, analysing data, or improving the company's online platforms.

You may also get to rotate through different roles to learn how tech interacts with various parts of the business.

Corporate support roles

In recent years, companies in this sector have recruited grads for their accounting & finance, HR, and legal departments.

Marketing roles

Marketing is a critical function of retail & consumer goods companies because of the high competition – every brand is vying for consumer attention, so companies need to differentiate themselves and marketing is an effective way to do that.

That's why out of all the sectors, the retail & consumer goods industry places the greatest emphasis on marketing and offers the most marketing graduate programs.

In a marketing-focused graduate program, you might get to work on projects related to product launches, market research, and customer retention.

R&D & engineering roles

Some companies in retail & consumer goods do their own R&D and manufacturing.

In this case, they'll need engineers to develop new products and improve processes at their factories, so if you have an engineering background, you can consider graduate roles in this sector too.

Roles at top companies in order of salary

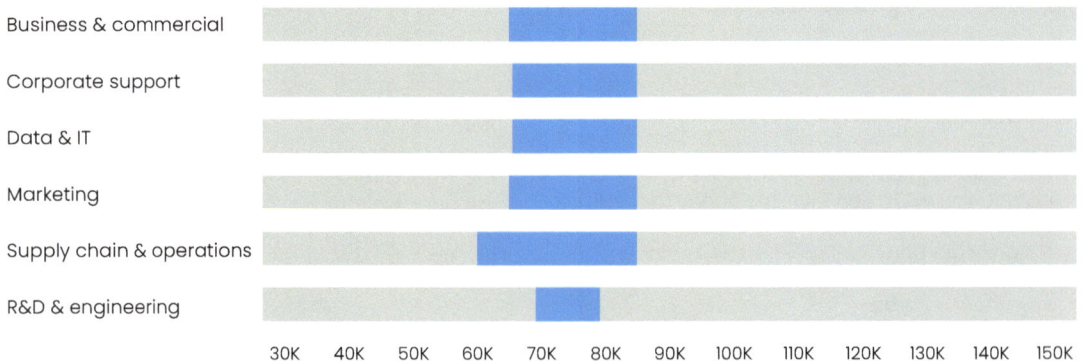

Business & commercial	~67K–85K
Corporate support	~67K–85K
Data & IT	~67K–85K
Marketing	~67K–85K
Supply chain & operations	~60K–85K
R&D & engineering	~67K–80K

Salary axis: 30K 40K 50K 60K 70K 80K 90K 100K 110K 120K 130K 140K 150K

Is it for me?

Do I need a relevant degree?

47%
of recent grads
in this sector studied
Business & management

Finance, accounting, economics & business administration	**13%**
Law, legal studies & justice	**11%**
Sciences	**9%**
Engineering & mathematics	**6%**
Other	**15%**

How much would I make?

Average pay by region

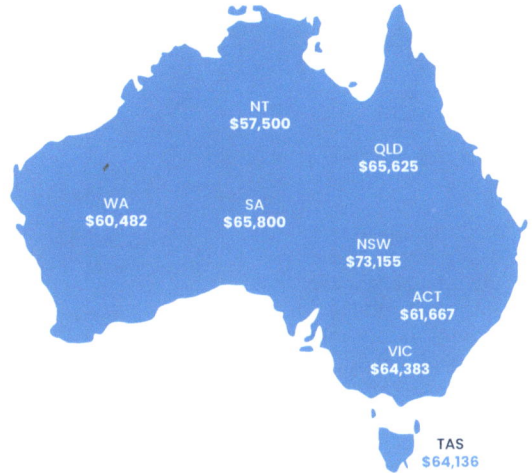

NT $57,500
QLD $65,625
WA $60,482
SA $65,800
NSW $73,155
ACT $61,667
VIC $64,383
TAS $64,136

Average salary

$59-$69K

Average hourly wage

$27.91

How much would I work each week?

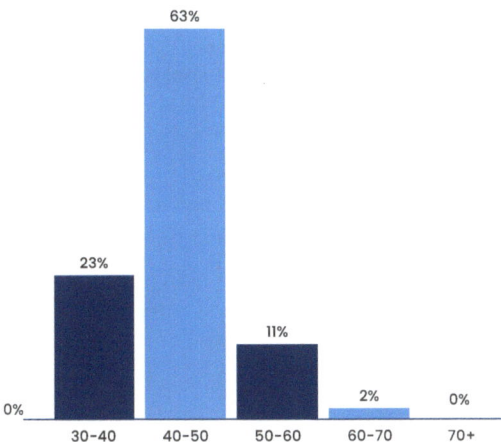

30-40	40-50	50-60	60-70	70+
23%	63%	11%	2%	0%

0% (before 30-40)

Would I enjoy the work?

- ☺ Flexible work arrangements
- ☺ Exposure to different areas and tasks
- ☺ Ability to own meaningful work
- ☹ Slow project time
- ☹ Lack of modern processes and equipment
- ☹ Lack of structure and process

Average rating

4.3
out of
5.0

★★★★☆

On the job

Will Stock

Bachelor of Banking and Finance; Monash University

Assistant Consumer Engagement & Data Marketing Brand Manager (Giorgio Armani & Yves Saint Laurent) at L'Oréal Australia and New Zealand

L'ORÉAL

'L'Oréal life is very fast- paced, which is what makes us who we are. A tight deadline is very conducive to fast learning.'

5:30 AM

WillyWeather showed minimal wind this morning so it's an early ride with some mates before work. This doubles as preparation for the weekly L'Oréal Cycling Club ride. Once toast and water have been consumed, I cruise down to the meeting spot and we enjoy the morning.

7:00 AM

Dead from my mates insisting 'it's just a hill' I return home, shower, and get ready for the day.

7:30 AM

Most of our graduate year has been at home, thus, I am very keen to get as much office time as I can! Seeing my teammates unpixelated is quite the treat. So, I race to the train and enjoy the morning read of what happened overnight, red, or green day today...

8:15 AM

I arrive at work and check my calendar, urgent emails from the night are replied to and/or information is provided. I check my to-do list and prepare for the rest of the day and week. I find this time the most productive as there are usually no meetings before 9 am. I can pull the data I require and start analysing without additional tasks jumping on my list. My manager is also an early starter so if anything urgent has risen we discuss.

9:00 AM

If we haven't caught up already my manager and I have our weekly WIP, we discuss the priorities for this week and chat about our weekends. My manager has not been able to make it down to Melbourne due to COVID, he is based in Sydney. Our team's skills have been constantly improving, but we are both itching to have the whole team together in person for the first time.

9:30 AM

I get stuck into the tasks I have for this week. Which promotions work best and why? If we clash with this competitor what will happen? Who is performing best in our markets and why? It is very interesting to deep-dive one of our competitors and find out what makes them tick, aka we monitor and predict their selling strategy. I look at all the information I can get my hands on, I then narrow it down to what is useful. The Category team is all about understanding the 'why'. Sales high or low we need to understand which factors we can control to maximise our ROI. Being a new grad learning new information systems has been quite challenging at times, but thankfully the team is always there to show me all the tips and tricks to maximise my productivity.

Scan to
read more
graduate stories

10:30 AM

I would normally join meetings with the different marketing team to discuss their proposed plans for next year or advise if any plans need to be changed this year based on the analysis the Category and Revenue Growth Management (RGM) team have done.

11:15 AM

I update any databases that need updating. This mainly deals with our internal planning tools so we can actively track future promo plans and forecasts.

12:00 PM

I open this week's catalogues for our primary retailers. Where our products appear, I take a screenshot and add to the weekly qualitative PPT I send out. I also collate the off-location imagery from the week that was. This adds depth to our quantitative analysis, off location compliance is highly valued so it is great to be able to visualise it too. Highlighting any points of note I send out to the whole division.

1:00 PM

Lunchtime/desk break! We are all encouraged to take a step away from our desk and enjoy lunch. A quick note through Teams to see which friends are ready for lunch. Time to go and enjoy the (hopeful) sun outside or the view from the top floor café.

2:00 PM

Learning webinar - throughout Melbourne lockdown, L'Oréal has offered us many upskilling webinars ranging from Microsoft Office advanced tutorials to yoga and fitness sessions. These are great for learning and keeping morale high whilst in and out of lockdown.

3:00 PM

You get a heads up that there are free products on another level. Yes, I would like to be the best son, brother, cousin, and boyfriend. So, I get in the elevator and race to where the products are. If the intel is good, you are one of the first people there. Win.

3:15 PM

Further quantitative analysis is continued, Youtube excel tutorials are watched, a formula I have never heard of is found.

4:00 PM

Most likely something urgent has arisen and takes priority over other projects. L'Oréal life is very fast-paced, which is what makes us who we are. A tight deadline is very conducive to fast learning. Once I have chatted it out with my manager and we worked out the best course of action. I completed the first stage and sent it to my manager for his thoughts. We optimise and work out the key points we want to pursue.

6:15 PM

I PowerPoint it up and make it look pretty (L'Oréal templates for the win). I shoot the final draft for my manager to sign off on.

6:30 PM

With tweaks noted, we are both happy and call it a night. The fun thing about being in the office during 2020/2021 is that we all must get out at around 6:30 PM when the disinfectant team comes in to spay every level.

7:15 PM

I get home and enjoy dinner with the fam. A sneaky game of Monopoly Deal usually follows – a great iso game would recommend. Enviably I don't win, real monopoly is more to my taste. After a few Youtubes (Sailing La Vagabonde and/or The Skid Factory) I'm ready for bed. Good night!

Technology

Photo courtesy of Macquarie Technology Group

The tech industry is the part of the economy that makes, sells, and supports all things related to 'technology' – but what exactly does that mean?

- If your mind wanders to **software** or **artificial intelligence**, you're on the right track, but just scratching the surface.

- Remember, tech extends to the realm of **hardware** too - the trusty servers that host your favourite websites, the smartphone that's practically an extension of your hand, and the tiny chips and circuits making it all tick.

- And let's not forget **the internet and telecommunications systems** which let us sling information around the world faster than you can say 'tech'.

There's loads more we could talk about - biotech, green tech, web3... the list goes on. For now though, just remember these key parts of the tech sector and you're good to go for your job search!

Where are the best places to work?

Sector Rank	Employer		Location of opportunities	Accepting applications from / Types of opportunities	Learn more
#1	Canva	**Canva** 4.3 ★★★★☆ #6 Overall	⊙ Sydney	B C E H I L M P S T Graduate jobs Internships	Page 136
#2	FDM	**FDM Group Australia** 4.1 ★★★★☆ #12 Overall	⊙ Sydney, Melbourne, Brisbane, Canberra	B C E H I L M P S T Graduate jobs	Page 139
#3	amazon	**Amazon** 4.2 ★★★★☆ #15 Overall	⊙ Sydney, Melbourne, Brisbane, Adelaide, Canberra, Auckland, Wellington, Remote	B C E H I L M P S Graduate jobs Internships	Page 141

The top companies in this space tend to fall into the following categories.

- **Software companies** make computer programs, mobile apps, and more – basically anything from the addictive games you play on your phone to the complex programs that keep global corporations running smoothly!

- **Internet companies** deliver a world of services and products right through your screen - think search engines, social media, and your favourite online shopping sites. Since most software these days is directly delivered through the internet, you'll often hear both software and internet companies lumped together under the term 'tech companies.'

- In the background are **telecommunications companies**, which make sure your calls go through and your internet connection remains seamless.

Photo courtesy of Macquarie Technology Group

- Rounding up the team, you'll find **tech consulting companies** – the problem solvers that help businesses set up, troubleshoot, and optimise their tech systems and digital operations.

What jobs are there?

Software development & engineering roles

Most tech jobs are in software development and engineering, which involve building software that meets the needs of users.

Developers primarily focus on coding while engineers take on a broader role, handling the overall architecture of a software system.

Cloud and networking engineering roles

Network engineers design the infrastructure that connects all the computers in a system, setting up routers and firewalls, and dealing with network outages.

Cloud engineers set up and maintain cloud services that allow companies to store their data online.

Data analyst roles

Data analysts process and analyse data, uncovering patterns in market trends and customer behaviour that help businesses make smarter decisions.

Security engineering roles

In a security role, you'd protect an organisation's information and systems from threats.

You'd design defences for databases, ensure IT security systems are in tip-top shape, look out for security concerns, and address breaches when they occur.

Tech consulting roles

As a tech consultant, you'd help businesses set up complicated pieces of software to best fit their needs.

Many tech consultants are business analysts who figure out clients' needs and keep projects on track and within budget.

Sales and business development (BD) roles

As a sales rep, you'd sell the company's products or services, with the goal of hitting specific revenue targets.

In BD, you'd have a more strategic role of scouting out new opportunities, partnerships, and ways for the company to grow in the long-term.

Either way, your mission would be to grow a company's customer base. (By 'customers,' we're mostly talking about other businesses, not individuals.)

Marketing roles

Tech roles that sell directly to consumers tend to have marketing roles.

Your tasks could range from collaborating with influencers to launching and tracking the performance of online ads promoting the benefits of a telco's network.

Corporate support roles

In recent years, leading tech companies have recruited fresh grads for their HR (also known as 'people & culture'), finance, and customer service departments.

Roles at top companies in order of salary

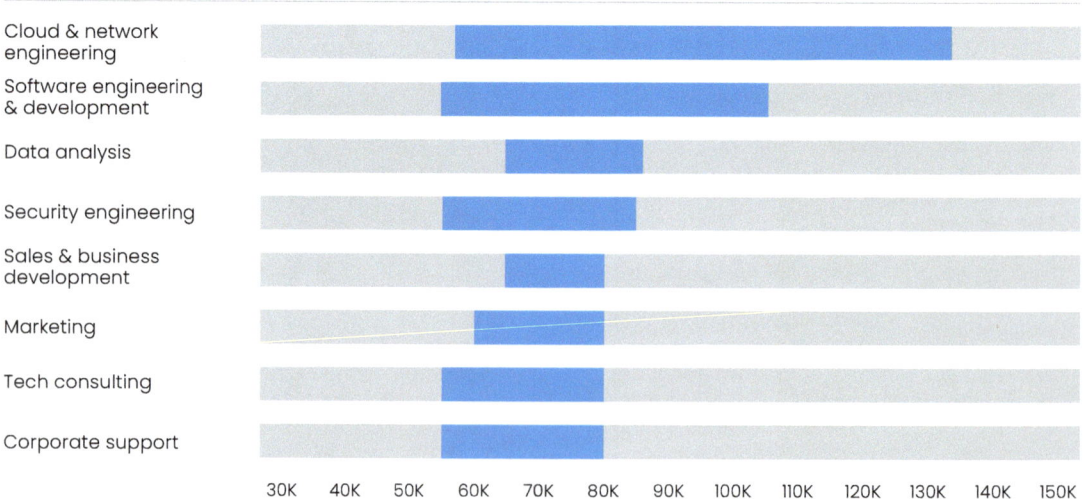

Cloud & network engineering	~55K–130K
Software engineering & development	~55K–105K
Data analysis	~65K–80K
Security engineering	~55K–85K
Sales & business development	~65K–80K
Marketing	~55K–70K
Tech consulting	~55K–80K
Corporate support	~55K–80K

30K 40K 50K 60K 70K 80K 90K 100K 110K 120K 130K 140K 150K

Is it for me?

Do I need a relevant degree?

41%
of recent grads
in this sector studied
IT & computer science

Engineering & mathematics	**21%**
Business & management	**16%**
Finance, accounting, economics & business administration	**7%**
Humanities, arts & social sciences	**5%**
Other	**10%**

How much would I work each week?

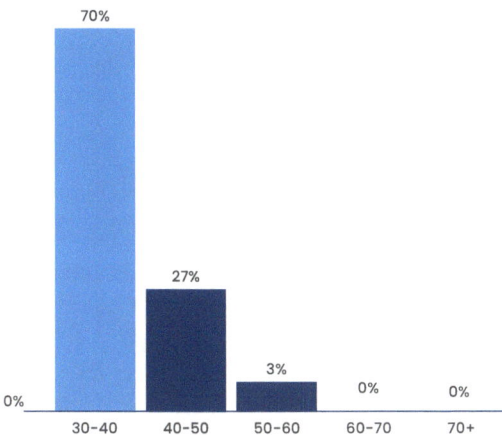

Hours	Percentage
30–40	70%
40–50	27%
50–60	3%
60–70	0%
70+	0%

How much would I make?

Average pay by region

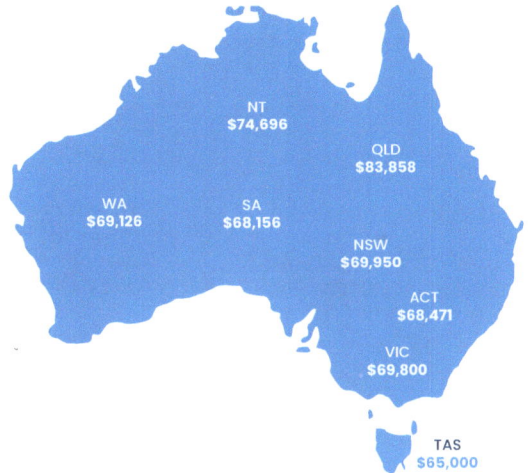

NT $74,696
QLD $83,858
WA $69,126
SA $68,156
NSW $69,950
ACT $68,471
VIC $69,800
TAS $65,000

Average salary
$64–$76K

Average hourly wage
$34.82

Would I enjoy the work?

- ☺ Good work environment
- ☺ Work-life balance
- ☺ Autonomy in roles
- ☹ Difficulty getting a raise
- ☹ Technical focus that may not allow for innovative integration of staff without IT background
- ☹ Lack of standardization in working ways

Average rating
4.4
out of
5.0
★★★★½

On the job

Vee Ciputra

Bachelor of Engineering
(Software Engineering);
University of Auckland

Graduate Frontend Software
Engineer at Canva

Canva

'This is one of the most exciting parts of my job; seeing how real users are enjoying (or struggling from) features that we've personally helped implement, and then taking the next step to further enhance their experience.'

What's your job about?

In simultaneously considering the 2 core missions of empowering design and doing good in the world, the company's main goal is to build a design product so impactful that opportunities for empowerment arise on a daily basis for millions of users. My part in this contribution is to help improve and enhance the frontend for Canva's Presentations.

Recently, I've specialised in enhancing the editing, viewing and presenting of Charts in presentations. This involves working alongside our team's Product Designers and Product Managers in order to deliver the highest quality features that bring the most value to our users. It's really rewarding that I get to interact with all kinds of people and be involved in the workflow of creating the product!

We usually start by focusing on goals for the team, and then assigning issues to whoever is keen to work on the task. During the task, there's usually a lot of design involved, so I always bother my team's Product Designer for some design advice and confirmations (shout out to Sam for doing such amazing work for the entire Presentations team!). Once I finish my implementation or bug fix, I create a Pull Request and get reviews on my code by other engineers. This is a great opportunity to learn about how I can improve my programming skills. Once it's approved, I get my feature signed off, and then it goes into production to be released into the world!

What's your background?

I was born in Indonesia, but I moved to New Zealand (that's right, not Sydney!) when I was 3, and have lived there ever since up until 2021 when I'll start my Graduate role at Canva in Sydney.

I'd always loved computers as a kid, and I got introduced to the fundamentals of coding at the age of 9 through Neopets.com! I learnt HTML and CSS, but unfortunately never went into coding after that as I focused on my school studies. In Year 12 (this would be Year 11 in Aussie standards) I realised I was sick of Science and I regained my interest in programming. Fortunately, I was completing subjects one year ahead of my current year, so in what was meant to be Year 13 (that's Year 12 for Aussie) I dropped out of high school to pursue Software Engineering in the University of Auckland.

Throughout my university career, I was the Marketing Coordinator for many clubs such as a Taiwanese social club (I'm not Taiwanese!) and TEDxUoA. More uniquely, my friends and I started up a brand new software club called Developers Society, which was the first non-exclusive tech club in Auckland. In the same year, we became the largest student-run tech club in New Zealand, and also won the UoA's New Club of the Year award. I'm super proud of that!

Canva was my dream job since I used it religiously for Marketing, so when I got an internship offer I was super stoked. Canva flew me over to Sydney and I had literally the best time, so I'm extremely excited to start my Graduate role in 2021!

Could someone with a different background do your job?

For sure! Software is so versatile and I believe you don't even need the highest qualifications as long as you have passion to learn and programme. I think the greatest thing about Canva is that almost everyone has different backgrounds, originating from different countries, experiences and degrees. It's all about loving problem-solving, loving people and loving the product that you're building (and in Canva's case, that's a given!).

What's the coolest thing about your job?

I love my role because it's so user-impacting, especially when releasing features that will be used by the world the next day. I've participated in several user-testing sessions (we call them Popcorn Sessions because they're very entertaining!) where I can see how real users interact with Charts and Presentations. This is one of the most exciting parts of my job; seeing how real users are enjoying (or struggling from) features that we've personally helped implement, and then taking the next step to further enhance their experience. Work is really meaningful because our efforts are genuinely impacting real users.

What are the limitations of your job?

Programming can be tedious, especially when you get stuck on a problem for a long time. Luckily, my Presentations team is super helpful, like the rest of the company, and is always willing to help overcome any blockers we face.

Another thing is that code reviews can sometimes be very gruelling, and I feel a lot of Imposter Syndrome, almost on a daily basis. Everyone is very talented and knowledgeable that I often feel inadequate - but the team is always very accommodating about this and always ensures that we are supported in moments like these. Reviews are learning experiences that help us improve!

3 pieces of advice for yourself when you were a student...

- Build relationships and make the most of your time with your friends and family, since you might move to a different country! It's important to enjoy your University years since you'll never get them back.

- Don't stress about grades so much. Grades are important, but they're not the key factors to your future and success.

- Take some time to work on personal projects and explore different technologies. You'll understand what other people are talking about a lot more, and you'll find your interests.

Photo courtesy of Macquarie Technology Group

prosple

Get a backstage pass of what it's like to work in a specific role

Read interviews and day-in-the-life articles from graduates and interns to get valuable insights into their roles, the company, their challenges, and the perks!

Photos courtesy of Clyde & Co, Kraft Heinz, Struxture, Macquarie Technology Group, and Prosple

SECTION 4

How to get hired

Your guide to a great career fair 108

7 tips for getting an internship 111

How to craft a winning CV...114

Your ultimate guide to psychometric tests 120

How to get an employee referral..124

How to ace interviews with the STAR technique 127

Your guide to a great career fair

If you've ever wondered whether career fairs are worth the hassle or how you could possibly stand out from the sea of students, we've got you.

But first, what are career fairs?

A career fair, also known as a 'job fair' or 'career expo,' is a gathering where employers meet with students like yourself. The goal? To provide information about their company and its opportunities – and scope out promising future interns and graduate employees!

Most universities host career fairs throughout the year. These events are often organised by the university's career services department or student organisations. So whether you're studying arts, sciences, business, or engineering, there's a good chance that a career fair is on your university's calendar.

Are career fairs worth it?

Career fairs are absolutely worth it – no, not just because of all the free swag you'll get.

If you already know what employers you want to apply to:

- **You can use career fairs to vibe-check the employer before applying:** Meeting employers at a career fair is a chance for you to check them out – before you go through all the work of applying.

- **You'll get face time with employers:** In an era where most of our job searches take place online, career fairs provide a rare opportunity to meet employers face-to-face and show them who you are beyond your CV. Leave a positive impression and you could land a job or internship down the line!

- **You can ask your most burning questions:** If you've found an employer you're interested in, chances are you have a bunch of questions for them. Career fairs are a great way to get those questions answered directly from the source.

Scan to **read online**

If you don't know yet:

- **You'll finally make that CV:** An upcoming job fair might be exactly what you need to finally crank out that winning CV.

- **You can sharpen your networking skills:** School doesn't prepare you to network or even hold a conversation in a professional setting. So use career fairs as your training ground!

- **You'll get free interview practice:** Just like interviews, career fairs force you to talk to employers in an uncomfortable setting. So treat them as a rehearsal before you're in the hot seat for real!

Plus, this may be the only time in your life when a career fair can help you land a job, so take advantage of it while you can!

How to stand out at a career fair

Here are five easy ways you can stand out at a career fair, according to recruiters and grads.

1. Look up the employers beforehand

Looking into employers beforehand is almost a guaranteed way to stand out from the crowd, because most people don't do it! They stroll up to an employer's booth and ask, 'So, what do you do?' or 'What jobs do you have for me?' These days, information like that is just a search away, so asking questions like these is like saying that you don't care.

Look up the employers online and decide which ones you want to meet. Then, research your target employers, making sure you know all about them and why you would want to work for them.

> **Hint:** You can check out an employer's profile on Prosple to get the low-down on them.

To help narrow down your options, you can also see which employers are actually hiring (Again, you can check their profile on Prosple to find out).

2. Arrive early

As the event progresses, recruiters start to lose their voices and – dare we say – a smidgen of their enthusiasm. So the earlier you go, the better!

3. Enjoy the conversation

At career fairs, students tend to be so nervous, they can't hold a normal conversation. So one simple way to stand out is to just be yourself. Chat with the recruiter like you might talk to a friend's parent.

At the entry level, most employers are gauging whether you're someone they could work with 40 hours a week. So just focus on having a conversation. They'll remember you for it – more so than the repetitive elevator pitches they heard from every other desperate student.

If you don't know know to make enjoyable conversation with strangers (aka 'networking'), use the career fair as practice!

4. Meet some employers who aren't on your list

It's easier to stand out when there's no competition. Check out some employers who don't have a ton of students waiting in line, and you might actually find a gem!

If you feel jittery, talking to these less popular employers is a good way to warm up. Use them to get comfortable and confident enough to be yourself. Then go approach your top choices!

5. Follow-up after the event

If you have a fantastic meeting with an employer during a fair but don't follow up, there's a strong chance they will forget you amidst the sea of students they spoke to at the fair.

So send a thank-you note to each recruiter that you met during the career fair. You can do this by dropping them an email or a message on LinkedIn along with an invitation to connect.

Go the extra mile for people with whom you shared the most memorable discussions, making sure to mention something unique to your chat that might help jog their memory. For example, if you mentioned a website you made, send a link to it in your follow-up message.

Scripts you can use during and after the career fair

Here's a formula for what to say when approaching an employer:

1. Introduce yourself
2. Say why you're interested in the employer and/or a specific role
3. Highlight relevant skills & experiences
4. Ask insightful questions that can't be answered from their website

Let's see this in action!

Here's what you might say if you're a business student interested in a marketing role

I'm Pat, a final-year business student. I've been keenly following [Employer Name] and I'm particularly interested in your graduate program in marketing. I've had hands-on experience leading data-driven marketing campaigns during my internship. Could you tell me more about the day-to-day responsibilities of a marketing grad at [Employer Name]?

And here's what you might say if you're a psychology student interested in an HR role:

Hey there! I'm Jamie, and I'm in the final stretch of my psychology degree. I've been really intrigued by [Employer Name]'s HR graduate program, especially because it aligns so well with my interest in workplace psychology and employee well-being. Could you let me know what skills and characteristics you look for in your ideal candidate?

Here's an example of what a Computer Science major interested in cybersecurity might say:

Hi there, my name's Alex. I'm studying Computer Science in my final year and I have a keen interest in cybersecurity. I've been following [Employer Name]'s work in this area for a while now and I find it really inspiring. I'm particularly interested in the ways AI can be used to enhance cybersecurity. Is that something [Employer Name] works on?

Scan to view more
samples of follow-up messages

What if I can't make it to an in-person career fair?

Employers also go to virtual career fairs, so you can check those out too. Here are our best tips –

- Dress to impress! Commit to professional attire from head to toe. While it's true that employers will only see your face, a confident demeanour shows even better when you put on a polished outfit. That's not something you can achieve with a pair of sweatpants.

- Choose a neutral background (real or virtual) with as few distractions as possible. You want the employer to focus on you and not wander through a myriad of things behind you.

- Pick up on non-verbal cues on when to ask questions, which usually happen towards the end of a meeting. Don't forget to look directly at the camera's lens from time to time. This is equivalent to maintaining eye contact.

But remember: even if you don't go to a career fair at all, you can still apply directly to an employer's jobs and internships here at Prosple.

Just try to make other opportunities to connect with people from the company – we promise, it'll be worth it.

7 tips for getting an internship without experience

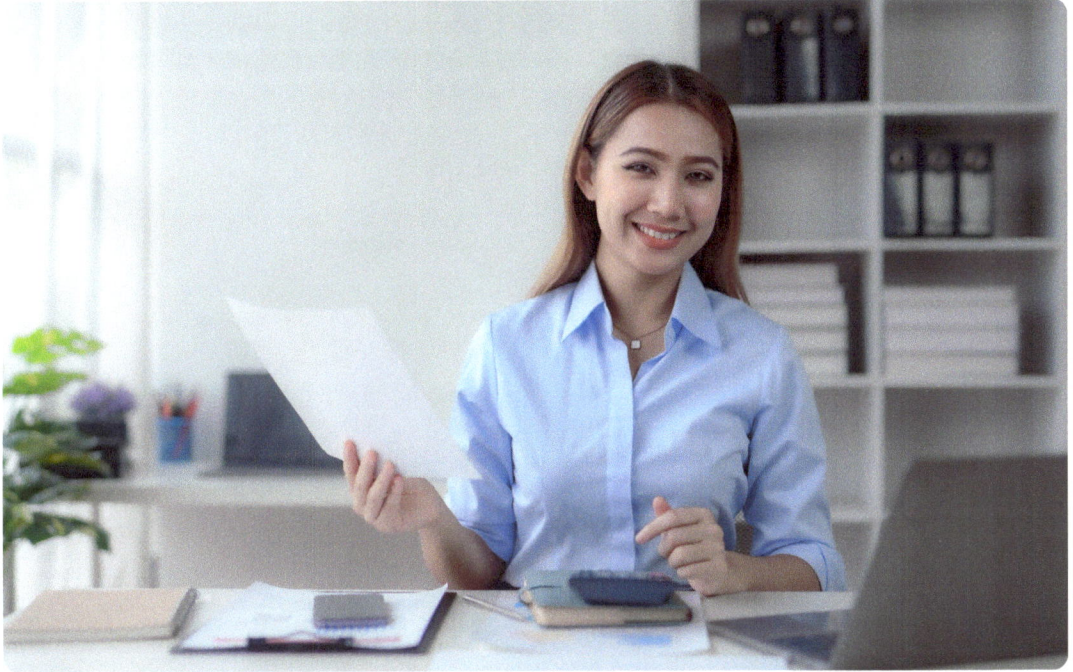

No experience? No problem! Check out our best tips for landing internships without any professional work experience.

First things first

But first, let's deal with the elephant in the room – do you need experience to land an internship? Luckily, the answer is 'no.'

> *'We're not expecting internship candidates to have had previous professional work experience. We don't expect you to have already worked as an engineer, architect or scientist - we know that an internship is designed to give you this experience, so don't stress about this.'*
>
> **– Graduate Recruitment Lead at GHD**

However, that doesn't mean you can send in a blank CV and call it a day! Notice the recruiter said they're not expecting 'professional work experience.'

In other words, while you don't need formal job experience in your chosen field, you still need to show that:

- You're serious about the company and role.
- You've got the potential to succeed.
- You're able to thrive in the professional world.

... and the more real-world experiences you have to show these things, the better!

1. Show you're serious about the company and the role

Here's how:

- Make sure you know enough to say what the company does (its core products & services), how they do it (their methods & technologies), and who they do it for (their target market or clients). After all, only then can you figure out how you fit in!

- Also ask 'How does the company make money?' This question will often uncover surprising insights into the company's strategy and direction.

- Look the company up in the news and ask your interviewer some questions about what you read.

- Research the company's mission and values.

Why this works

- Nearly 80% of employers expect applicants to know about their organisation according to the Australian Association of Graduate Employers. Yet this is where many students fall short.

- From the employer's perspective, if you're not serious about the company now, how can you be serious about it after you get the internship?

- And let's be real: If you don't have relevant experience, it helps to at least show that you're serious … not applying on a whim!

  'An understanding of [our company] shows that a candidate has done prior research and indicates a genuine interest in our company and business.'

  – Recruitment team at FDM Group Australia

2. Show that you're passionate about the industry

Here's how

- Find hands-on ways to demonstrate your passion. Participating in business case competitions or managing the finances of a student club say much more about you than saying 'I'm passionate about business.'

- Regularly write on LinkedIn about new things you learn about the industry.

- Join industry-related clubs or online forums to engage with professionals. If there aren't any related clubs at your school, start one!

- Attend workshops and seminars to continually develop your knowledge and skills.

- If you're majoring in something totally unrelated to the degree, highlighting relevant coursework can help convince recruiters of your interest.

Why this works

- Whether it's engineering or human resources, passion for a specific field often translates into motivation, creativity, and a willingness to go the extra mile – all things that recruiters like to see.

3. Get to know recruiters

Here's how

- Go to industry events and career fairs to meet recruiters.

- Connect with them online and send them a personalised follow-up message expressing your interest in the company.

- Keep in touch with them by commenting on relevant content they share on LinkedIn or emailing them – just don't be pushy in your approach.

Why this works

- Recruiters get hundreds, if not thousands, of applications. So meeting them in person – and staying in touch – can help them put a face to your application.

4. Highlight relevant projects

Here's how

- If you've done any school projects or side projects that showcase skills that would be useful for the internship, don't be shy about bringing them up!

- Focus on projects that are unique. For example, everyone who's taken an intro software programming course has probably made a timer app. So make something that goes beyond the basics.

- Detail the projects on your CV, focusing on your role and the skills you used. Then relate the projects to the internship's responsibilities in your cover letter and interview.

- Create a portfolio to demonstrate your work and share it during the application process.

Why this works

- One of the biggest concerns recruiters have when hiring students is the uncertainty about whether you can translate the skills you've learned into the real world. Working on pet projects shows that you can do just that!

- Projects also show that you didn't just take classes (which anyone can do) - you care enough to work on your skills in your free time.

- This tip works well for tech jobs – after all, there's nothing more convincing to a tech recruiter than an app or software program that actually works.

- But really it's the case for almost any job out there. Whether it's a marketing campaign you designed for a class, a community event you organised, or even a personal blog you write, these experiences can set you apart from other candidates and provide tangible evidence of what you're capable of.

5. Show that you can learn quickly

Here's how

- Provide examples of how you've adapted to new challenges, learned a new skill, or improved a process quickly.

- After your interview, ask for feedback. For example, you could say something like 'This is one of my first times interviewing. Would you be able to provide any honest feedback or thoughts on how I did? I'd really appreciate your insights for my own personal development reasons.'

Why this works

- Most companies prefer fast learners. They're quicker to train, and therefore less costly for the company.

- Failing that, they'll hire junior folks who are at least keen to learn. So show you can take feedback, adapt, and learn on the fly.

6. Show that you've got soft skills

Here's how

- Think about what soft skills the role requires. (Hint: The job description is a good place to start).

- Use specific examples to demonstrate how you've applied these skills in the past. For example, if you're trying to show you've got teamwork skills, don't just say you were on a

sports team; share an anecdote about being a team player.

- It is totally OK to draw from your experiences working part-time jobs, student clubs, or volunteer activities as long as they help you make a convincing case for your soft skills.

Why this works

- At the junior level, employers don't expect you to have too many hard skills. They know that soft skills are way harder to teach … so if you've got 'em, make sure to flaunt 'em!

7. Show that you can get things done

Here's how

- Whenever you bring up an experience (e.g. in your CV, cover letter or interview), focus on showing how you 'got things done' – this means highlighting not the tasks you performed, but the impact you achieved.

- Another way to think about this is to focus on achievements that are unique to you.

- For example, let's say you worked a retail job during uni. If you bring it up in your application, don't dwell on your day-to-day tasks ('I stocked shelves, operated the cash register, and assisted customers') – anyone who's ever worked in retail could say that! Instead, mention how you boosted sales (e.g. 'Recognized as Top Salesperson of the Quarter for consistently exceeding sales targets by 20%').

Why this works

- In the world of working professionals, you'll always be measured by your ability to get things done and contribute to their organisation – that's why people hire you in the first place and why they give you bonuses and raises later on.

- Focusing on specific achievements allows you to present yourself as a capable and results-driven individual, even without a traditional employment background in the field.

Scan to **start exploring opportunities**

How to craft a winning CV

The ultimate guide to CV-writing for students and graduates!

In most cases, your CV will be the 'first impression' that a potential employer has of you. This makes it the single most important document for getting your career started. Unfortunately, your CV is probably also one of the most difficult and time-consuming documents to get right.

Fear not: We've compiled the ultimate guide to help you put together the perfect CV for internships and grad jobs!

1. Why do CVs matter?

But first, why are CVs so important? Let's step into the shoes of an employer for a moment.

Employers get loads of applications for each job and can't interview everyone. Just think, if a manager had to interview thousands of people for each opening, they'd have no time left for their actual work!

That's where CVs come in. They help narrow down the list to those candidates who look promising enough for an interview. A well-crafted CV can catch an employer's eye and spark their interest in getting to know more about you.

So, your CV is not just a formality—it's your ticket to an interview. If your CV doesn't stand out, you might miss your shot at an interview. That's why a good CV is so important.

2. How do I make my CV stand out?

Wondering how to make your CV pop? It's all about staying on point. Think about it like this: When you're telling a story, do you include every single detail? Probably not!

Treat your CV in the same way. Instead of boring recruiters with everything you've ever done, pick out the highlights. Remember, the goal is to make it easy for recruiters to quickly understand your qualifications and decide if you're a good fit.

Here's a simple way to go about this.

- **Look at the job ad:** What skills and qualities are they asking for? Write those down.

- **Match it up:** Next to each item from the job ad, write down your skills, experiences, and achievements that show you've got what they need.

Scan to **read online**

Now you've got a list of what to put on your CV!

3. How long should my CV be?

Your CV should ideally fit onto one A4 page, or two pages at the absolute max. Anything more than that will likely frustrate the recruiter – they review dozens of CVs each day and won't have patience for a multi-page essay.

4. How should I structure my CV? What information should I include?

Most CVs can be organised into the following sections:

a. Heading & contact details
b. Summary (optional)
c. Education
d. Experience
e. Additional (optional) sections, which can include:
  • Interests / Extracurricular activities
  • Awards & accomplishments
  • Skills & attributes

Let's jump in and take a closer look at each section!

a. Heading & contact details

The main heading should simply be your name. You don't need to include 'CV'. Recruiters know what they're reading!

Immediately under (or next to) your name, you should include your contact details. This includes:

• **Your phone number** so that recruiters can easily reach out to clarify anything. Make sure any phone voice messages on the number you provide are professional – no 'Hey, You've reached my number. I'll call back when I feel like it! Jkjkjk lol!'

• **Your email address.** Remember to spell your email correctly (no '@gmail.cmo's') and avoid 'humorous' email addresses (no 'ninjapizzalover@email.com' please!).

In addition, you can also include:

• **Your location.** Simply specify your city or region (e.g. Sydney, Australia). Your full address is not needed until you've been officially hired.

• **Links to your professional online profiles** (assuming they are suitable for prospective employers!), such as your LinkedIn, Twitter, Github (if you're a developer), or personal website.

In some parts of the world, it is standard to include personal details like your age, gender, date of birth, marital status, and number of dependents. Do not do this in Australia. It's actually unlawful for employers to ask you about most of these things as per regulations set by the Australian Human Rights Commission.

b. Summary (optional)

Scan to **view samples of summaries** you can add to your CV

c. Education

Employers don't care about education as much when hiring experienced candidates. But when you're just starting out? It's what you should put at the top of your CV. Here's what you absolutely must include in this section:

• **University & degree.** As a grad, your degree gives employers an idea of what skills you might have. For some roles, you may even be screened out based on your degree alone, so make it easy to find on your CV!

• **Start & completion dates** (or expected completion dates). Include the month and year. This lets employers know whether you're still a student and when you're available to start working, among other things.

Here are some extra things you can put in this section — assuming they make you look good and are relevant to the role!

- **School results:** If you got good grades, like a 6.0 GPA or higher, show them off! This can show you're hardworking or really good at what you study. If you're looking for jobs in other countries, help them understand your grades by explaining what they mean, like 'High Distinction (86 out of 100)', '6.7 Grade Point Average (max 7.00)', '73 GAMSAT score (98th percentile)'.

- **Coursework:** Generally, you should only delve into subject-level detail if it's relevant. For example, if you're applying for an internship at an accounting firm without an accounting degree, you could still get hired if you highlight that you've done well in relevant courses like business law, financial planning, and data analytics.

- **Your high school:** Include your high school and any notable achievements — like a high ATAR (>85), leadership roles, or any awards — if they might demonstrate diligence and intelligence.

- **Academic awards, research projects, and dissertations.**

- **Training, licenses, or accreditations,** e.g. micro-credentials or industry certifications.

- **Study abroad experience** if applicable.

Do NOT feel a need to include any of the above if they aren't relevant or would reflect poorly on you. Remember: Your CV is meant for you to show off your strengths!

d. Experience

Your education matters, but it's not enough to get you a job. After all, you're not the only student with a degree from your uni! What'll help you really stand out (and land that interview!) are the things you've done and experienced. That's what the Experience part of the CV comes in.

What to include

Your professional experience may be limited. Fortunately, most graduate employers are aware of this and look favourably on achievements that have taken place outside of traditional work settings.

That's why we recommend calling this section 'Experience', instead of just 'work experience'! Examples worth mentioning include:

- voluntary positions
- fundraising positions
- contributions to University clubs, societies or other membership bodies
- roles in sporting organisations
- freelance assignments
- part-time work
- internships
- temporary gigs

Again, you don't need to list every experience you've had. Instead, focus on highlighting experiences that are relevant to the position you're applying for. A CV where each item screams 'I'm the one!' is far more impactful than a CV that's all over the place.

For each experience, include:

- Your job title — put this first since employers want to know what you did.

- The organisation name. If the name doesn't clearly indicate the kind of organisation it is, you may need to include a sentence or two that describes it.

- Your start and finish dates (month & year is fine).

- A short description of what each experience involved, focusing on facts that are most relevant to the role.

Scan for the **full guide** on what to put in your experience section

What order to put your experiences in

When it comes to arranging your experiences on your CV, you've got a couple of choices.

1. **Reverse chronological order (most recent first):** This is the traditional and most widely used format. It lists your experiences starting with the most recent and working backwards. It's straightforward and preferred by many employers as it clearly shows your career progression.

2. **Order of relevance:** If you don't have a clear career progression (e.g. you've jumped around and tried out different things), lead with your most relevant experiences, regardless of when they occurred. Think about it like this: If you start with less relevant experiences, there's a

risk a busy recruiter might miss the good stuff and overlook your CV.

How to describe your experiences

You should aim to include enough context that an uninformed reader (someone who doesn't have prior knowledge of you, your area of study, or your industry) can grasp what you did and why it makes you qualified for the job.

For each experience, include a high-level overview of your role and responsibilities. You can also include a few bullet points that cover specifically what you accomplished, learned or contributed. You may find the 'STAR' framework (Situation, Task, Action, Result) helpful for teasing out these details:

- Describe a situation (i.e. the position you occupied or a challenge that you faced)

- Explain the task you had to do

- Clearly outline the specific actions you took to complete the task

- Finally, describe the results and what you accomplished, learned or contributed

Here are a few tips to help you along the way:

- **Make your experience relevant.** Highlight why each experience is relevant to the role you're applying for. For example, don't just say you 'worked in a bar'— describe how working in a 200-person capacity venue required exceptional customer service, dispute resolution skills, excellent time management or any other qualities the employer is looking for.

- **Emphasise your achievements.** Don't just list out your duties & responsibilities. Employers want to know if you did a good job. For example, don't say 'managed [student association's] social media accounts' – anyone can do that. Instead say that you 'elevated [student association's] online presence by managing their social media accounts, resulting in a 30% increase in follower engagement within six months.'

- **Quantify your impact:** Use numbers to highlight your actions and results. Specify things like how much, how often, how long, and how many to paint a clear picture of your impact.

- **Make it about you.** If you say you were 'involved with' a project, employers might assume you played a minor role. To convey your active involvement, use action verbs like 'designed', 'built', and 'organised' and provide specific examples of how you solved a problem, took the lead on something, or significantly contributed to a successful outcome.

- **Keep it simple.** It's tempting to use industry jargon to look smart. But often, the first person to read your CV won't be an expert. They'll most likely be a recruiter, hiring for all kinds of roles across their organisation (e.g. marketing, sales, finance, engineering, etc). If they can't make sense of your CV, they'll often just skip it. So keep your CV easy to read and interesting for anyone!

- **Avoid empty buzzwords.** Vague, subjective terms like 'self-starter', 'effective communicator', 'works well under pressure' are chronically overused, and overreliance on them can result in your CV coming across as a list of meaningless buzzwords. If they're important to your role, try to demonstrate these attributes in your bullet points by using tangible achievements.

e. Additional (optional) sections

If there's extra space on your CV and you want to showcase more about yourself that isn't covered in your Education or Experience sections, consider adding these details towards the end of your document.

Common additions for students and graduates include:

- Awards & accomplishments
- Activities & interests
- Skills & attributes

Remember, these sections are entirely optional. Only include them if they add value to your profile (e.g. help round you out as a candidate) and are relevant to the job you're applying for.

5. What design and layout should I use for my CV?

Design might seem like a big deal, but most employers aren't looking for fancy CVs.

Actually, unless you're applying for a design role, there's no need to make a CV from scratch. Most people just use ready-made templates, and recruiters are cool with that.

So, take it easy and stick to a template. Here are some free ones to help you out. When you're choosing, think about:

- **The industry:** Traditional sectors like finance or law often prefer classic, more conservative styles – think: black text on white paper.

- **The company vibe:** If the place you're applying to is all about new ideas and being different, then you can try something a bit more modern and creative.

- **How much you've got to say:** Got loads of achievements and projects to talk about? You'll need a template that fits all your info without looking squashed. Skip those super sparse ones with lots of empty space.

If you decide to tweak a template or make your own, here are some things to keep in mind.

- **Headers:** Headers are titles that mark the start of different sections on your CV, such as 'Education,' 'Experience,' and 'Skills.' Use a bigger font size and/or color to make them stand out so recruiters can find what they need quickly.

- **Bullet points:** Instead of writing paragraphs, break things down into short, snappy points. Each bullet point should be 1-2 lines max. Recruiters usually don't have time to read big blocks of text on a CV!

- **Font: Use a simple and clean font like Calibri or Arial.** Keep the size between 11-12 so it's easy to read — 10 at the smallest. You don't want anyone squinting!

- **Bold words:** If you know a job is looking for certain skills, make those words stand out in bold: e.g. 'Experienced in **Java** and **Python**'.

- **White space:** Don't pack every inch with text. A bit of empty space makes your CV easier on the eyes and less crowded.

- **Widows and orphans** (if your CV is longer than one page): Avoid having single lines of text stranded at the top or bottom of a page. It's like when a sentence gets cut off and continues on the next page of a book — annoying, right? Keep your ideas together, so they're easy to follow.

Scan to **download CV templates** you can use

6. Steps to review and finalise your CV

- **Always ask someone else to read over your CV.** You'll be amazed at the typos a friend or family member can catch. And if you're applying for a role that requires you to be detail-oriented (e.g. a quality control role), you'd better make sure there aren't any mistakes in your CV!

- **Ask for additional feedback from your university's careers service center.** Most universities offer a free CV review for current students.

- **Once you're happy with the final version, save the file as a PDF.** Give your PDF a professional title (such as 'Jane Smith CV').

- **Do a final FINAL review of the PDF version before you submit it.** And make sure you upload the correct version!

Good luck!

7. FAQs

Scan for **more tips and FAQs**

a. Should I include a picture on my CV?

No. It adds no value, and some recruiters will explicitly request that candidates NOT share pictures, so as to avoid any risk of unconscious bias.

b. What file type should I use?

Unless directed otherwise, always submit your CV in PDF format. Why? The hint is in the name - 'Portable Document Format'.

This format 'freezes' your desired formatting in place, so your document displays in the same way regardless of the software, hardware or operating system that recruiters use to view your CV.

There are many websites that'll let you convert documents into PDF format for free. Alternatively, you can use Google Docs to create your CV and download it as a PDF for free.

c. Should I include references in my CV?

No. Most reference checks will only be done at the end of the recruitment process, and recruiters often complete them using an online workflow, so there's no benefit to taking up valuable space on your CV with references.

The only exception to this is if you have a particularly influential referee and you feel it will help your case to 'name drop' them on your CV.

Don't bother writing 'references available on request'. It goes without saying that you would provide references if an employer asked for them.

d. Do I need to tailor my CV for each employer?

No. Employers in the same industry tend to look for similar qualities, so you can just use one CV for the whole industry.

However, if you're applying for different roles in the same industry, you'd still want to modify your CV to highlight experiences that best match the job description for each role.

Pro tip: Create a 'master' version of your CV that covers everything. This allows you to select appropriate content from the master version as a starting point for each position and employer.

e. Should I use certain keywords to pass the automated CV check?

No. Automated CV checks are mainly a myth at this point. We've not yet heard of an employer taking this approach – and for good reason.

There are stringent employment laws promoting fair hiring practices, and AI tools have been shown to have strong biases up to now. (A case in point is when Amazon had to abandon their AI screening tool for penalising CVs mentioning 'women'.)

That said, using the same keywords from the job ad can help. This is because recruiters often aren't experts in the field they're hiring for, so seeing familiar terms from the job description can make your CV easier for them to understand.

Just remember to use only keywords you can justify. If you stuff your CV with all the keywords from the job description, it could make employers feel like you're trying to trick the system rather than showing your real skills. And if they doubt your honesty, they won't consider you for the job.

f. Can I get ChatGPT to write my CV for me?

Nope, don't let an AI tool write your whole CV. As an employer ourselves, we can assure you that it's painfully obvious when someone outsources their application to ChatGPT!

If you do use an AI writing tool, use it wisely. For example, you can ask ChatGPT to brainstorm keywords to include or to edit your CV for clarity, relevance, and impact. Just don't get it to generate a CV without putting any thought into it

g. Can I lie on my CV?

No, lying on your CV is not a good idea because: Recruiters are skilled at spotting things that don't add up. They talk to lots of candidates and are good at telling when something is off. If they find out you're not being truthful, they won't trust you anymore.

Before giving you a job, employers will check your references. That means they'll contact the professors or bosses you said you've worked with. If your stories don't match up, they'll know something's wrong.

Plus, the professional world can be small. People talk, and a lie can follow you around, making it hard for you to get a job later on. It's always better to be honest and show what you can really do.

h. Can I put special requests on my CV?

No, do not mention requests for things like special working hours or days off. It's best to cover this in your interview.

Scan to **view samples** of winning CVs

Your ultimate guide to psychometric tests

Don't wing your psychometric tests. No, really, don't.

About psychometric tests

What are psychometric tests?

Psychometric tests are like quizzes that help reveal what you're like, how you think, and how you might act in different situations. These tests get their name from two Greek words: 'psycho,' meaning mind, and 'metric,' meaning to measure.

The psychometric tests you'll encounter will most often take the form of a timed, online test where you might:

- Answer questions about your personality.
- Choose the right word to complete a sentence.
- Spot the pattern in a group of shapes.

Think of it as a brain-teaser. For instance, if you see a couple of rows of shapes that follow a pattern, could you figure out what the next shape should be? That's the sort of challenge these tests might throw at you.

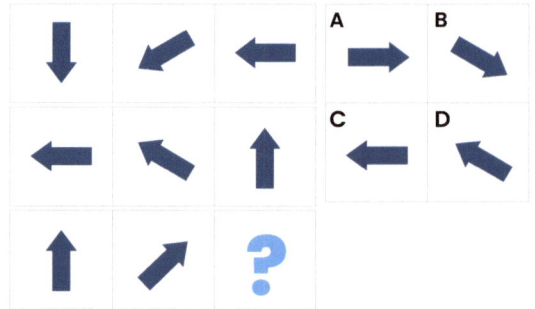

Why are psychometric tests used in job applications?

In theory, psychometric tests allow employers to:

1. **Look beyond skills and experience:** While a candidate's skills and experience are important, they don't show everything about a person. Psychometric tests help employers understand hidden qualities that aren't obvious from a CV, such as how well someone manages their emotions or solves problems.

2. **Ensure the candidate fits the job:** Employers want to find someone who not only has the right skills but also thinks and feels in ways that match the job and company culture. Psychometric tests help them see if a candidate's personality and thinking style are the right fit for the role.
3. **Create equal opportunities:** Psychometric tests are used to give all candidates a fair chance. The idea is that no matter where you come from or who you are, the test will measure everyone by the same standard, making the hiring process more objective and unbiased.

Prosple's take on psychometric tests

In practice, the main reason large employers use psychometric tests is to streamline their screening process. Flooded with applications, they turned to psychometric tests as a way to quickly decide which candidates to interview.

Ironically, this isn't what the tests are actually meant to do. In the hiring process, psychometrics are meant to give a more complete picture of a candidate outside of CVs and interviews – not serve as the initial filter that narrows down the applicant pool.

Here at Prosple, we also have some reservations about the accuracy of psychometric tests. To put these tests to the test, we had our entire team complete two of them. The results were, let's say, eyebrow-raising.

- Take one of our team members—a university prize-winning writer with stellar communication skills. Surprisingly, she scored low on the verbal reasoning section of the intelligence test!

- When it came to the personality test, what people said about themselves didn't always align with their workplace behaviour.

So why would some of the biggest organisations in the world rely so heavily on psychometric testing? We believe their choice boils down to a mix of efficiency and pragmatism.

- Sure, there are more accurate ways to gauge job performance, like task-based assessments. But those options come with a time and resource cost that's often not feasible at scale.

By comparison, psychometric tests are quick and easy: They're created and run by external testing companies so employers don't need to lift a finger.

- Plus, large companies aren't exactly short on applicants. So, for them, it's less about snagging every potential superstar and more about finding a reliable method that sorts the wheat from the chaff without taking an eternity.

So prepare well for your psychometric tests, but don't take the results too seriously. They are not a reflection of who you are or how well you'd do at a job.

But more on this later! Let's first dive into how you can ace these tests.

How to ace your psychometric tests

1. Get to know the tests

That's right – psychometric tests aren't just one test. They're actually a mix of different tests that check things like your personality, maths skills, and logical thinking skills. Get to know each kind so you're ready for anything on test day!

Numerical reasoning test

- **Assesses:** How good you are with numbers -- including how well you perform calculations, interpret graphs and tables, and make logical deductions based on numerical information.

- **Sample question:** 'Here's a graph displaying sales figures for different products over a period of time. Calculate the percentage increase in sales for a specific product between two given months.'

Verbal reasoning test

- **Assesses:** How good you are at working with written information -- meaning how well you understand written passages, draw logical conclusions, and make accurate inferences.

- **Sample question:** 'Which of the following statements is most supported by the information in the passage?'

Logical reasoning test

- **Assesses:** Your logical thinking abilities are -- for example, how well you identify patterns, make logical deductions, and draw accurate conclusions.
- **Sample question:** 'Here is a series of shapes. Which shape comes next in this sequence?'

Personality test

- **Assesses:** Your personality - including your communication style, work preferences, and how you might fit into a team or organisational culture.
- **Sample question:** 'Rate how much you agree or disagree with the following statements: (1) 'I enjoy being the center of attention' (2) 'I prefer working alone rather than in a team."

Situational judgment test (SJT)

- **Assesses:** How well you handle a variety of workplace situations. The point is to see how you'd respond to real-life work scenarios, whether you fit the company culture, or have solid decision-making abilities, people skills, etc.
- **Sample question:** 'You've been working on a project for several weeks, and it's due in two days. You realise that there's a significant error in your calculations, which will affect the final outcome. Which of the following courses of action would you take?'

Scan to **view sample questions** on these tests

Depending on the industry or organisation you're applying for, there may be other types of tests. In recent years, a handful of organisations have started using games to assess candidates. In the accounting job industry, candidates might face specific psychometric tests designed to assess their proficiency in data analysis. These tests are tailored to evaluate the ability to interpret financial data, understand complex charts, and make logical deductions.

So make sure to scope out what kind of tests you're up against! If the employer doesn't provide much information on this, you can find out by searching online or looking in online platforms such as Whirlpool, Reddit, and Glassdoor.

2. Think from the employer's perspective

For the personality and situational judgment tests, one 'hack' is to think from the employer's perspective. For instance, a personality test might be 'How regularly do you pay your bills on time?' Even if you're always late with your bills, answer 'often' or 'very often' – you don't want employers to think you're irresponsible!

Or let's say you encounter this situational judgment problem:

Situation: You've been working on a project for several weeks, and it's due in two days. You realise that there's a significant error in your calculations, which will affect the final outcome.

Options:

1. Correct the error yourself, work late if needed, and hope no one notices the mistake.
2. Immediately inform your team and supervisor about the error and work together to fix it.
3. Present both the incorrect and corrected versions during the project review, explaining the mistake openly.
4. Document the error and the correct version, then ask for an extension to redo the project.
5. Blame the error on a software glitch and proceed with presenting the incorrect data.

Each option can tell the employer something different about you.

1. If the company values individual accountability, option 1 could be seen as taking initiative, though it carries the risk of not solving the problem in time.
2. If the company values transparency and teamwork, they might look favourably on option 2.
3. Option 4 would likely be appreciated in a culture that values thoroughness and quality over deadlines.

Understanding the company culture and what qualities they value can help you navigate which response would be seen as most favourable. And if you don't know what they're looking for, check the employer's profile on Prosple, the employer's website, or ask the recruiters!

3. Pace yourself

Time management is crucial for any exam, but it's particularly key for psychometric tests. Here's a simple strategy. Before diving into each section:

1. Note the time limit.

- Give yourself the best chance of landing a job or internship of course!

Recommended resources:

- **Employer-provided practice tests:** If you're given a practice test, work it until you could ace it in your sleep. No practice test? Search for samples online.

- **Careervidz' tutorials on Youtube:** These tutorials show how to solve quickly. Check out their psychometric test playlist to get started.

- **Paid services:** Need extra guidance? There are paid services like the Psychometric Institute in Australia that offer specialised courses.

5. Rest up

Last but not least, make sure you're well-rested before test day. You'll be able to think more clearly and work through more problems when your brain is fresh and energetic!

What to do if you keep failing psychometric tests

If you keep failing psychometric tests even after you follow all our advice above, it's not the end of the world. There are some very smart, successful people who'll never pass these tests because of reasons like ADHD, severe test anxiety, or other factors.

If you fall into this category of people, rest assured. There are plenty of employers out there who don't require psychometric testing! These will tend to be smaller organisations and start-ups, who go through much fewer applications and therefore:

- Can spare more time on each candidate, which means they don't need a psychometric test to screen you out.

- Can't afford to miss out on a real gem who just can't sit exams.

What next?

However you feel about psychometric tests, you'll be taking a lot of them, so we hope these tips help you maximise your scores!

2. Divide the total time by the number of questions to figure out your average time per question.

This will help you gauge how much time to spend on each question. Being aware that you have, for example, 10 seconds per question stops you from lingering too long on tough questions and missing out on easier ones. Each question is worth the same amount of points, so if you find yourself going overtime on a question, take your best guess and move on.

But don't fret if you can't finish every question. These tests are designed to stretch your abilities, not gauge whether you can answer every single question. No one completes them all. So keep your cool and just focus on doing your best!

4. Practise, practise, practise

Do not wing your psychometric tests. You might be tempted to think of psychometric tests as just another test, but they're not.

You'll want to practise the exams in order to:

- Familiarise yourself with the format and the time constraints, so you can walk into the actual exam with confidence.

- Identify your strengths and weaknesses and focus your efforts on the areas you need to work on. For example, in accounting jobs, this will mean improving your grasp of complex financial regulations or enhancing your proficiency with accounting software.

How to get an employee referral

Learn how an employee referral could get you noticed by recruiters – and how you can secure one!

First off, what's an employee referral?

A referral is a recommendation from someone within the company or connected to the company where you're applying. This individual vouches for your qualifications, skills, and suitability for the position.

Typically, the person referring you knows you personally or professionally and can attest to your work ethic, character, and abilities.

Referrals are basically like someone inside the company giving you a thumbs up and saying, 'I know this person, and they would be a great fit here.'

Why should I get an employee referral?

Reason #1: Most recruiters love referrals – especially when it comes to students & grads

Recruiters see employee referrals as the 2nd most popular source of quality candidate.

From the recruiter's perspective, the only thing better is an 'internal hire' – that's when a company recruits someone from a different part of the company.

But internal hires are practically non-existent for students and grads, so employee referrals are basically your best bet for being noticed.

Reason #2: Referrals can boost your chances

While referrals don't guarantee you the job, they usually do increase your chances of landing the job – or at least an interview.

Great, now how do I get an employee referral?

There are a few different approaches to getting an employee referral depending on whether you already have personal connections to the company and how much time you have before the application.

Scan to
read online

If you already know someone at the company

- Always check your personal network first! Does a friend, classmate, family member, or former coworker work at the company?

- From a recruiter's perspective, referrals from people who actually know you carry the most weight – especially if they're someone you've worked with before.

- If nobody in your immediate network works at the company, you can also try asking the people they know – i.e. a friend of a friend, a friend's parent, a parent's friend, you get the gist.

If you don't know anyone at the company & you've got time

If you don't know anyone at the company and neither does anyone in your network, your best bet is to find employees to connect with, build relationships with them, and then ask for referrals.

1. **Identify potential contacts**
   Look for employees within the company who share common interests or backgrounds (e.g. alumni from your school), have similar roles to the one you're interested in, or are involved in projects that resonate with your skills and passions.

2. **Build relationships with them**
   Building a relationship takes time and effort, so be patient and authentic in your interactions. Here are a few ways to do this

   a. Follow them on professional platforms like LinkedIn and engage with their posts in online forums. This shows genuine interest and can spark a connection.

   b. a personalised message and express interest in them (their career and their role). Ask for general insights or advice rather than jumping straight to asking about the company.

   c. Request a short (e.g. 30-minute) call to ask them about their career. Most likely, if they're a recent grad or intern, they'll be flattered!

   d. Continue to engage with them over time, sharing relevant content, asking thoughtful questions, and offering value in return.

3. **Ask for the referral when appropriate:** Once you've established a connection and have a better understanding of each other's professional interests and values, you may feel comfortable asking for a referral. Be sure to explain why you think you're a good fit for the role and how their endorsement would be meaningful.

By this point, they're almost guaranteed to offer you a referral!

If you don't know anyone and you're running out of time

But we get it, you don't always have the time for all that, so here's a simplified process:

1. Identify potential contacts
2. Reach out directly, express interest in their career, and request an informational interview
3. After the chat, request a referral

And if you really don't have time, you can skip to asking for the referral from the get-go. This is the option with the lowest chance of success, but it does occasionally work. Here's how you make it happen:

Personalise your approach

Send a personalised email or message explaining why you're reaching out and how you know them – you can say that you've been following them on LinkedIn for a while or that you admire their work.

Give them context

Explain the role you're interested in and why you believe you're a good fit. Ask if they would feel comfortable referring you.

Provide support

Provide your resume or other supporting materials and offer to discuss your qualifications further if they would like more information.

What do I say to get a referral?

Here are some samples you can use as a basis for your own requests.

Sample #1: Phone call to a family friend

I was chatting with [Family Member's Name] the other day, and they mentioned that you work at [Company Name].

I've been researching the [specific position] there, and I'm really excited about the opportunity. It seems like a fantastic fit for my skills and interests.

Listen, I was wondering if you might be willing to refer me for the position? I believe that my experience in [mention relevant experience or skills] aligns well with what they're looking for and I'd really love it if you could vouch for me … but no pressure obviously!

Scan **to view more sample scripts** for calls and messages

What else should I know about referrals?

How do referrals work?

Traditionally, a referral involves someone walking your resume over to HR. These days, it can take many forms.

- Your referrer might submit your resume through a special portal within the company's hiring system.

- You might submit the application yourself with a referral code.

If the company asks you to email your application materials, you can write in the email header 'Referred by so-and-so.'

Whatever the case, the HR department or hiring manager usually prioritises your application, knowing that you come with an internal stamp of approval.

Then, assuming you land the job or internship (or meet some other metrics), your referrer might get a financial bonus or other incentives, such as additional vacation days or gift cards.

Can I get a referral after I've applied?

- Yes, you can still get an employee referral after you've applied.

- In some companies, the referral process is integrated into the recruitment system, allowing current employees to vouch for candidates at any stage of the application process.

- At other companies, an employee may not be able to refer you in the computer system, but can still contact the recruiter or hiring manager to make a case for your application.

- The main difference is that the referrer won't get a referral bonus. This is because the bonus is meant to encourage employees to identify talent that might not otherwise apply – and if you've already applied, then they're technically not 'referring' you to the company!

Do I need a referral from someone high up in the company?

Nope, just focus on getting a referral!

Can a referral get me a job I'm not qualified for?

No, a referral just helps move your application towards the front of the line. If you're not qualified, this just means getting rejected sooner! In this case, your time is better spent getting qualifications instead of a referral.

Can an employee referral hurt your chances?

Referrals generally don't hurt your chances of landing a graduate job or internship. That is, unless perhaps the person referring you has a negative reputation within the company.

However, there are cases where a referral won't help. This may be because:

- A company doesn't have a referral policy.
- Too many people get referrals.

Different offices of the same company may even have different policies. When in doubt, ask the recruiter!

How to ace interviews with the STAR technique

The STAR method is a proven way to ace interviews. Learn how to use it like a boss.

Scan to **read online**

With competition for internships and entry-level jobs at an all-time high, it's important to make a strong impression during your interview. Enter the 'STAR method' – a guaranteed way for you to showcase the thing many interviewers look for in entry-level hires: potential for excellence.

What is the STAR method?

The acronym STAR refers to:

- **S**ituation
- **T**ask
- **A**ction
- **R**esult

Although its origins are largely unclear (several sources attribute the mainstreaming of the technique to Amazon), the STAR method is a popular technique that helps interviewees frame their responses to questions in a succinct and specific manner.

What interview questions can you answer with the STAR method?

The STAR method is specifically for answering behavioural interview questions also known as experience-based or scenario-based questions. As the name implies, behavioural questions do not

test your technical knowledge of the role. Rather, they are a way for interviewers to get a sense of who you are as a person, your work ethic and your attitude in the workplace.

By asking behavioural questions, recruiters use past behaviour to predict future success. This is why the STAR method is crucial as an answering technique for these types of questions.

How to identify behavioural questions

Typically, you can spot behavioural questions by the following prompts:

Describe a time when…

Can you give us an example of…

Tell us of how you dealt with…

Have you ever been faced with X situation? How did you handle it?

What did you do when…

While not all behavioural questions use the same prompts, they'll generally ask you to recount past experiences or situations to provide an answer. These questions are designed to gauge your ability to handle different work scenarios and demonstrate your behavioural patterns.

policy or SOP for the task, refer to it first (but briefly) and then talk about how you specifically implemented those processes.

Also, showcase your skills by using strong action verbs. For example, instead of saying 'I helped with the project,' say 'I spearheaded the project.' Don't be afraid to put yourself in the spotlight.

Just don't go overboard! Remember to strike a balance between providing enough detail to showcase your skills and actions, and being concise enough to keep the interviewer engaged.

Result (10%)

You've talked about what happened (Situation), what needed to be done (Task), and what you did (Action). Now it's time to talk about the outcome of your actions; the result(s).

The Result section is an underrated but critical part of the STAR method. As one grad at the Commonwealth Bank puts it, 'The R for 'results' is very important. Treat this part like every self-reflection in your assignments/life experience.'

As much as possible, lean into numbers as a way of quantifying your results to your interviewer. For example, instead of saying, 'As a result of my leadership skills, the project was completed on time,' say 'As a result of my taking initiative and suggesting we delegate xyz portion of the project to abc team, we not only completed the project one week ahead of time, the project also helped drive the company revenue 15% higher than the previous years.' Be specific and provide measurable impact that demonstrates how YOUR actions led to success for the entire company.

What are some examples of the STAR method?

Question 1: When was a time you took a risk and failed? How did you respond? How did you grow from it?

- **Situation:** There was a time during my previous job as a marketing specialist when I was responsible for launching a new product that our company had invested a lot in. There was a lot of pressure because we had already set these ambitious targets for our sales and profits.

- **Task:** To ensure that we would meet our targets, I decided to take a risk. At the time I believed this campaign would generate a high return on investment and help us achieve our sales targets so I decided to invest a significant portion of our advertising budget into a digital campaign.

What are the four steps of the STAR method?

Situation (20%)

The Situation section is not only the first step but also the foundation of the STAR method. Think of it as answering the question, 'What happened?'

While you want to give as much context as necessary, try to keep this part to 20% of your overall answer or less (think: 2-3 sentences). Set the background to the story and move on.

Task (10%)

After you've provided enough background information for your interviewer, the next step is to describe the task at hand.

A simple way to frame your task answer would be to answer the question, 'What exactly needed to be done in this situation?' or 'What was the goal?' Also remember to keep it brief, preferably 1-2 sentences.

Action (60%)

The Action section is the 'star' of the STAR method. It should form the bulk of your response because it highlights your role in bringing about the final outcome of the situation.

The main emphasis in this section is YOU. What did YOU do? What steps did YOU take? What decision(s) did YOU make?

Be as detailed as possible here. If you took four different steps to achieve the end goal (task), outline them step-by-step. If there was a company

- **Action:** However, things didn't go as I had hoped. Our engagement and conversion rates were lower than what we had projected, and we didn't meet our sales targets either. But instead of dwelling on the failure, I immediately took responsibility for making the decision that cost us and then organised a team meeting to assess what went wrong in the campaign strategy. We analysed the data collected from the campaign and identified the areas that needed improvement.

- **Results:** Although the campaign was not successful, it provided valuable insights into our target market and the effectiveness of our marketing strategies. By analysing the data and taking an open and honest approach to evaluating our mistakes immediately after, we were able to develop a more effective marketing plan for the next quarter. In the end, the failed campaign helped us grow as a team by encouraging reflection and constant improvement in our work.

Question 2: Tell me about a time when you had multiple important projects to finish and how you prioritised them.

- **Situation:** As a team lead in my previous marketing role, I was usually responsible for managing multiple time-sensitive campaigns. There was one week I had three urgent requests that needed immediate attention and were all of equal importance.

- **Task:** One project involved creating targeted email marketing campaigns, the other was on designing new product packaging, and the third was updating our social media marketing strategy. Each one was crucial and timely so I knew I had to find a way to handle them concurrently.

- **Action:** To do this, I started by assessing the priority level of each task by looking at the timelines and client expectations. Then I delegated tasks with a focus on the most urgent project. I made sure I communicated these priorities to my team members and created a project schedule and timeline so everyone knew exactly what needed to be done and by when.

- **Results:** By effectively prioritising these three projects, we were able to meet the required deadlines and achieve successful outcomes for each of them. The targeted email marketing campaign saw a 25% increase in click-through rates, while the new product packaging design helped in clarifying the product's features to our clients, and after updating the social media marketing strategy, we achieved a 20% increase in conversion rates. All of this was possible through team effort and it made us more efficient moving forward.

Question 3: Tell us about a time when you had to work in a diverse team to accomplish a project. What kinds of issues arose and how did you address them?

- **Situation:** When I was a marketing student at the University, I had the opportunity to work on a group project where I had to collaborate with a diverse team. My group consisted of fellow students with diverse backgrounds and skill sets.

- **Task:** Our assignment was to develop a comprehensive marketing plan for a local startup that would effectively promote the startup's product and differentiate it in the market.

- **Action:** To make the most of our differences and bring them all together in our work, I took the initiative of organising regular meetings where we could all share our insights and perspectives on the task. It was all about open dialogue and collaborative brainstorming in those sessions. Because we had these different opinions and approaches, there were moments when disagreements popped up. But whenever that happened, I made sure we had discussions to find common ground. The goal was to reach a consensus and keep our team dynamic positive.

- **Results:** At the end of the project, our strategy of highlighting our diverse perspectives paid off. We turned in a well-thought-out marketing plan that covered various channels and strategies despite our limited professional experience. We all earned an A in the course and to top it off, our Professor was very impressed with our work.

Scan to **view more questions** and how to answer them

What are the advantages and disadvantages of using the STAR method?

Advantages of using the STAR method

You provide clearer and more concise answers to the questions asked: The STAR method is a structured approach to answering interview questions. It covers the key points interviewers look for to make the right decision. Working through each step of the STAR method forces you to think through complex situations and craft a concise and focused answer while effectively conveying your experience and highlighting your competencies.

You come off as more confident during interviews: An added plus of using the STAR framework to provide more concise answers is that you come across as better prepared and more confident. Hiring managers are always looking for candidates who present themselves in a professional and organised manner and so the STAR method is crucial if you want to make a strong impression.

You get a confidence boost: The reflective nature of the STAR method can help you overcome your interview fears. Because you need to look back on your past achievements to craft your Situation-Task-Action-Results answers, you become more aware of how far you've come and why you deserve any interview opportunity. This might just be the confidence boost you need!

Disadvantages of using the STAR method

You run the risk of sounding robotic: The STAR method provides a structured approach to answering interview questions, but over-relying on it can make you sound scripted and less authentic.

To avoid this, use bullet points to highlight key details instead of memorising a script. For example, you might centre your interview responses on KPIs (key performance indicators) or other key metrics from your previous roles, focusing on examples that demonstrate your strengths and qualifications.

Also, be spontaneous and adapt your responses to the natural flow of the conversation. Use vivid language and sensory details to make your response more memorable.

Blending structure with spontaneity and authenticity is key to using the STAR method effectively.

How to use the STAR method to prepare for interviews

1. **Identify all your career highlights (both accomplishments and challenges faced)**
   It's likely you'll need to recall different experiences to answer the behavioural questions you'll be asked. If you're worried that you don't have enough professional experiences to draw from, look to your university experiences. Recall volunteer roles, group projects, and positions you held and outline both your accomplishments and challenges.

2. **Narrow down to your five best career stories**
   To increase your chances of success in interviews, use the STAR method and narrow down to your five best career stories that align with the KSAs (Knowledge, Skills and Attributes) required for the job.

   Read the job description carefully and note the skills, responsibilities, and requirements sought by the employer. Choose five stories that best reflect your abilities in those areas. Also, make sure your stories are aligned with the core values of the organisation you're applying to. This will demonstrate to the interviewer that you understand their company culture and are a great fit for their team.

3. **Reframe these stories for a variety of different questions**
   All you need are five strong stories with multiple perspectives to answer different questions. For instance, if you have a story about a difficult problem you faced at work and how you solved it, you can use this story to answer questions related to leadership, teamwork, decision-making, and conflict resolution. By being able to reframe your stories, you always have strong, relevant examples to draw from regardless of the direction of the interview.

4. **Practise your answers and do mock interviews**
   The most effective practice is done by simulating an interview setting. You can ask a friend, family member, or career counsellor to conduct a mock interview with you. When doing mock interviews, make sure to dress up as if you were attending a real interview, and use a timer to ensure that you stay within the allotted time frame for each question. As you answer each question, remember to break up your answer into Situation-Task-Action-Result. Over time, you'll be able to fine-tune your response and improve your confidence.

prosple

Australia's **top100**

GRADUATE EMPLOYERS

Get to know
Australia's Top 100
Graduate Employers

Australia's Top 100 Graduate Employers

#1 Capgemini Australia and New Zealand

4.8 ★★★★★
#1 in Management consulting

Accepting applications from* B C E H I L M P S T

Types of opportunities Graduate jobs | Internships

Location of opportunities ⊙ Sydney, Melbourne, Brisbane, Adelaide, Hobart, Canberra, Auckland, Wellington, Christchurch

WHAT IT'S LIKE?

Shannon D'Souza
Associate Consultant

I've found to culture to be quite welcoming and engaging. At Capgemini, you are in control of your own experience. I mean that you choose the training you do, the side projects that you involve yourself in, and how you engage with the client.

REVIEWS

☺ 'We are really well taken care of and pushed to be the best version of ourselves.'

☺ 'You are free to work from home or in the office as you please. Work hours are generally flexible.'

Read the full interview and more reviews at 🚀 au.prosple.com

#2 NAB Australia

4.6 ★★★★⯪
#1 in Banking & financial services

Accepting applications from* B C E H I L M P S T

Types of opportunities Graduate jobs | Internships

Location of opportunities ⊙ All over Australia, work from home

WHAT IT'S LIKE?

Nemi Safieddin
Business Banking Graduate

The coolest thing about my job is having a direct impact on a customer getting the loan they require. It's a great feeling to see something get approved after putting hours of work in. I was also flown to Sydney to do a workshop with several other members of the graduate cohort which was a great experience!

REVIEWS

☺ 'I have made some of my best friends at work. There is a very welcoming culture.'

☺ 'My managers are/have been accessible and we also have the option to participate in a mentoring program.'

Read the full interview and more reviews at 🚀 au.prosple.com

*key for degrees where they accept applications from on page 7

#3 Deloitte.

Deloitte Australia
`4.2` ★★★★☆
#1 in Accounting & advisory

Accepting applications from*   B C E H I L M P S T

Types of opportunities   Graduate jobs   Internships

Location of opportunities   ⦿ Sydney, Western Sydney, Melbourne, Perth, Brisbane, Adelaide, Canberra, Hobart, Launceston, Darwin

WHAT IT'S LIKE?

Melissa Bandara
Climate and Engineering Graduate

The Deloitte graduate program helped set me up for success from my very first day at Deloitte. The program provided a seamless transition from university life to the world of consulting. Consulting training, network opportunities and continuous support from my team were all pivotal in making my transition successful.

REVIEWS

☺ 'Flexibility, the people, and learning opportunities.'

☺ 'The people I get to work with and also the type of clients I get to work on I find are the best thing about my job.'

Read the full interview and more reviews at
🚀 **au.prosple.com**

#4

Commonwealth Bank
`4.4` ★★★★☆
#2 in Banking & financial services

Accepting applications from*   B C E H I L M P S T

Types of opportunities   Graduate jobs   Internships

Location of opportunities   ⦿ Multiple locations in Australia

WHAT IT'S LIKE?

Evangeline
Technology Graduate

As a grad, I liked the ability to rotate into different teams. I'm building a knowledge base and taking it with me to my next role from each team. People in the team put an emphasis on how you're a fresh set of eyes and encourage you to bring new ideas in. I've always received feedback from every idea I've brought in, nothing was ever shut down by the business.

REVIEWS

☺ 'Pay is competitive and on the higher end of the offers I received for the graduate intake.'

☺ 'A great culture where everyone is really supportive of graduates and willing to take the time to teach you.'

Read the full interview and more reviews at
🚀 **au.prosple.com**

key for degrees where they accept applications from on page 7

#5 Optiver ▲

Optiver

`4.5` ★★★★⯪

#1 in Trading

Accepting applications from*	B E I S
Types of opportunities	Graduate jobs · Internships
Location of opportunities	⦿ Sydney

WHAT IT'S LIKE?

Suganya Suresh
Software Developer

At a Graduate level here, the level of ownership is huge. There's a focus on doing great development work and delivering something on time that solves a real business problem that we're facing. I also like the people. It's a friendly place to work.

REVIEWS

🙂 'Excellent pay and perks. Good culture, friendly colleagues and reasonable work life balance.'

🙂 'Everyone is really smart, really interesting, and really driven. Coming to work feels kind of like when I started going to university with the number of different ideas floating around.'

Read the full interview and more reviews at 🚀 **au.prosple.com**

#6 Canva

Canva

`4.3` ★★★★☆

#1 in Technology

Accepting applications from*	B C E H I L M P S T
Types of opportunities	Graduate jobs · Internships
Location of opportunities	⦿ Sydney

WHAT IT'S LIKE?

Jerome Han
Data Science Intern

We come to work everyday with the unique opportunity of leveraging cutting-edge research in machine learning to help solve problems and empower the world to design.

REVIEWS

🙂 'Very flexible... The company trusts that employees will 'be good humans' and do their best work'

🙂 'There are various Canva clubs which provide great opportunities to get to know other Canvanauts.'

Read the full interview and more reviews at 🚀 **au.prosple.com**

key for degrees where they accept applications from on page 7

#7 PwC Australia

pwc

3.7 ★★★★☆

#2 in Accounting & advisory

Accepting applications from*	B C E H I L M P S T
Types of opportunities	Graduate jobs Internships
Location of opportunities	⦿ Australia

WHAT IT'S LIKE?

Stacey Kent
Consultant (Financial Advisory - Corporate Tax)

Within PwC itself, there're ample opportunities to create the career you want to be based on your evolving skills, so if there're elements from your current role you'd like to delve more deeply into, you can find the opportunities and support to do this.

REVIEWS

☺ 'I have been so lucky to have the most supportive team and make some lifelong friends so early in my career.'

☺ 'Work flexibility and free coffees. As well as the never-ending possibilities to expand my career.'

Read the full interview and more reviews at 🚀 **au.prosple.com**

#8 Oliver Wyman Australia & New Zealand

4.0 ★★★★☆

#2 in Management consulting

Accepting applications from*	B C E H I L M P S T
Types of opportunities	Graduate jobs Internships
Location of opportunities	⦿ Melbourne, Perth, Sydney

WHAT IT'S LIKE?

Nick Vernon
Senior Consultant

You really can forge your own career path at Oliver Wyman, and the firm is very focused on development. The people I've worked with here have some important common traits—they're curious, humble, straight-talking, and always supportive of one another. They also know how to have fun as a team.

REVIEWS

☺ 'Amazing office and great amenities.'

☺ 'Great office culture, friendly people, interesting work, rapid pace of learning and quick development, great perks, competitive salary.'

Read the full interview and more reviews at 🚀 **au.prosple.com**

key for degrees where they accept applications from on page 7

#9 **ARUP**

Arup
4.7 ★★★★★
#1 in Engineering consulting

Accepting applications from*	B E H I M P S T
Types of opportunities	Graduate jobs Internships
Location of opportunities	⊙ Adelaide, Canberra, Melbourne Maroochydore, Perth, Sydney, Brisbane, Gold Coast, Cairns, Townsville, Canberra, Sunshine Coast

WHAT IT'S LIKE?

Jason Michael
Graduate Engineer

Arup's flexible working opportunities allow me to spread my working hours across the office and home to maintain a healthy work-life balance.

REVIEWS

☺ 'Provide graduates with lots of learning opportunities.'

☺ 'There are clear targets around hiring and retention of women in a male-dominated industry, and it makes a huge difference, with ~50-50% gender balance in the office.'

Read the full interview and more reviews at 🚀 **au.prosple.com**

#10 **IMC** TRADING

IMC Trading Australia
4.5 ★★★★★
#2 in Trading

Accepting applications from*	E I S
Types of opportunities	Graduate jobs Internships
Location of opportunities	⊙ Sydney

WHAT IT'S LIKE?

Anna Hardy
Trader

IMC, despite being externally competitive, is internally collaborative so any achievements or losses are shared between everyone. The flat structure at IMC also means a great idea can come from a 6-month grad or a 5-year trader. We all have a strong work ethic but keep work entertaining.

REVIEWS

☺ 'IMC provides many employee benefits and care about the well-being of their employees.'

☺ 'The people are great! It's a super collaborative environment which makes it perfect for learning as a grad.'

Read the full interview and more reviews at 🚀 **au.prosple.com**

*key for degrees where they accept applications from on page 7

#11 KPMG Australia

KPMG

3.9 ★★★★☆

#3 in Accounting & advisory

Accepting applications from* B C E H I L M P S T

Types of opportunities Graduate jobs Internships

Location of opportunities ⊙ Sydney, Melbourne, Canberra, Brisbane, Gold Coast, Perth, Adelaide, Darwin, Hobart, Parramatta, Wollongong, Geelong, Townsville

WHAT IT'S LIKE?

Timothy Bourke
Consultant

What I love most about working at KPMG is the networking opportunities. Whether it's a client or other people around the office, it's always interesting to get to know other people from all walks of life.

REVIEWS

☺ 'Managers are readily accessible and are always there to provide mentorship and teach you.'

☺ 'Office space and facilities are fantastic and provide you with everything you could possibly need and more.'

Read the full interview and more reviews at 🚀 **au.prosple.com**

#12 FDM Group Australia

FDM

4.1 ★★★★☆

#2 in Technology

Accepting applications from* B C E H I L M P S T

Types of opportunities Graduate jobs

Location of opportunities ⊙ Sydney, Melbourne, Brisbane, Canberra

WHAT IT'S LIKE?

Shevon Lau
Technology Migration and
Integration Consultant

With the support from my trainers, peers and account managers, I was able to overcome my self-doubt and achieve so much more than I could've imagined.

REVIEWS

☺ 'Great environment, everyone is equal, always down for a laugh.'

☺ 'Everyone I interact with from FDM that I would consider a manager is good value, easily accessible and pleasant to work with.'

Read the full interview and more reviews at 🚀 **au.prosple.com**

*key for degrees where they accept applications from on page 7

#13

GHD

`3.9` ★★★★☆

#2 in Engineering consulting

Accepting applications from*   B C E H I L M P S T

Types of opportunities   Graduate jobs   Internships

Location of opportunities   ⊙ Australian Capital Territory, New South Wales, Northern Territory, Queensland, South Australia, Tasmania, Victoria, Western Australia

WHAT IT'S LIKE?

Patrick O'Neill
Water Engineer

I've had the opportunity to see things I've designed to be constructed, and have worked on projects that have impacted the water and wastewater systems that I use in my day-to-day life.

REVIEWS

☺ 'Great mentoring - Amazing team & people - Senior employees motivate young graduates to push themselves - Interesting & variety of work.'

☺ '...the team wants everyone to have the best opportunities they can and support each other to produce the best results.'

Read the full interview and more reviews at 🚀 au.prosple.com

#14

L'ORÉAL

L'Oréal Australia & New Zealand

`4.2` ★★★★☆

#1 in Retail & consumer goods

Accepting applications from*   B C E H I L M P S T

Types of opportunities   Graduate jobs   Internships

Location of opportunities   ⊙ Melbourne, Auckland

WHAT IT'S LIKE?

Nathan Dickson
Marketing Management

The best part of my job is how much responsibility I'm given as a graduate. We're seen as future leaders of the business and are given really interesting projects to work on.

REVIEWS

☺ 'The company provides plenty of resources and guidance to allow not only progression in your current field, but the ability to make career moves across divisions and functions.'

☺ 'Everyone very supportive of your learning and development as a graduate and welcoming into the company.'

Read the full interview and more reviews at 🚀 au.prosple.com

key for degrees where they accept applications from on page 7

#15

Amazon
`4.2` ★★★★☆
#3 in Technology

LEARN MORE AND APPLY NOW!
scan to visit their profile

Accepting applications from* B C E H I L M P S

Types of opportunities Graduate jobs Internships

Location of opportunities ⊙ Sydney, Melbourne, Brisbane, Adelaide, Canberra, Auckland, Wellington, remote

WHAT IT'S LIKE?

We strongly believe that the best outcomes come from embracing a variety of perspectives, so at Amazon, we really embrace individual expression, show respect for different opinions, and work together to create a culture where each of us is able to contribute fully.

REVIEWS

☺ 'Managers are accessible, and understanding when you need time off etc.'

☺ 'Corporate discounts with airlines, Bose headphones and more. Public transport commuters subsidy. Phone bill subsidy.'

Read the full interview and more reviews at 🚀 **au.prosple.com**

#16

WSP Australia
`4.2` ★★★★☆
#3 in Engineering consulting

LEARN MORE AND APPLY NOW!
scan to visit their profile

Accepting applications from* B C E H I L M P S

Types of opportunities Graduate jobs Internships

Location of opportunities ⊙ Australia wide

WHAT IT'S LIKE?

Kate Lipczynski
Undergraduate Engineer - Power Team

Having an Indigenous background in engineering is very important to implementing these projects effectively in the communities in which they are located. I can add value by improving general cultural awareness and sensitivity, as well as encouraging the dialogue between the client and the communities.

REVIEWS

☺ 'Work-life balance, friendly and supportive coworkers and managers.'

☺ 'Abundant training resources, exposure to projects to develop the knowledgebase. Structured program to end as a autonomously working professional.'

Read the full interview and more reviews at 🚀 **au.prosple.com**

key for degrees where they accept applications from on page 7

#17 BHP

BHP
4.2 ★★★★☆
#1 in Mining, oil & gas

Accepting applications from* B E H I L M P S T

Types of opportunities Graduate jobs Internships

Location of opportunities ⦿ Queensland, South Australia, Western Australia

WHAT IT'S LIKE?

Rachel Fong
Integration Lead

My job is always changing, sometimes in the most unpredictable way but that's what I thrive on! It gives me the autonomy and 'seat at the table' to drive solutions to our tactical and strategic problems across all areas of how we work, so we can get better every day.

REVIEWS

☺ 'As a grad, I am getting on the job training with good salary and bonus. Deals on accommodation/care hire etc.'

☺ 'Their commitment to mental health.'

Read the full interview and more reviews at 🚀 **au.prosple.com**

#18 ANZ

ANZ
4.4 ★★★★½
#3 in Banking & financial services

Accepting applications from* B C E H I L M P S T

Types of opportunities Graduate jobs Internships

Location of opportunities ⦿ Sydney, Melbourne, Perth, Adelaide, Brisbane

WHAT IT'S LIKE?

Luke Kelly
Graduate Experience Designer

ANZ offers excellent career prospects for its graduates. At the end of the program, there's a guaranteed job offer waiting for you.

REVIEWS

☺ 'The positive culture and their dedication to your learning.'

☺ 'The variety of work that is undertaken, exposure to different industries, networking opportunities just to name a few'

Read the full interview and more reviews at 🚀 **au.prosple.com**

key for degrees where they accept applications from on page 7

#19 KEARNEY

Kearney
4.2 ★★★★☆
#3 in Management consulting

Accepting applications from* B C E H I L M P S T
Types of opportunities Graduate jobs Internships
Location of opportunities ⊙ Sydney, Melbourne

WHAT IT'S LIKE?

Sakilan Gopalarajah
Senior Business Analyst

The people are what make problem-solving fun, make our social events enjoyable, and keep your spirits up even when facing the toughest problems.

REVIEWS

☺ 'Flexible/hybrid working modes combined with travel opportunities.'

☺ 'Everyone at the firm will support you in achieving your career goals; there is a strong development focus.'

Read the full interview and more reviews at 🚀 **au.prosple.com**

#20 coles group

Coles
4.2 ★★★★☆
#2 in Retail & consumer goods

Accepting applications from* B C E H I L M P S T
Types of opportunities Graduate jobs
Location of opportunities ⊙ Victoria

WHAT IT'S LIKE?

Anthony Tripodo
Marketing Graduate

Coles has a flexible working policy which allows you to work flexibly based on how you work best. There have been days that I've worked from home or readjusted my start/finish time to allow me to do everyday life admin. It's as simple as talking to your leader to find what is best for you and the business.

REVIEWS

☺ 'Coles is focused on conscious inclusion in recruitment, and always seeks to support people based on their needs. I cannot fault them at all in this area.'

☺ 'As a graduate, I am involved in decision-making and feel as though I have genuine autonomy.'

Read the full interview and more reviews at 🚀 **au.prosple.com**

*key for degrees where they accept applications from on page 7

#21

Nous Group
`4.3` ★★★★☆
#4 in Management consulting

LEARN MORE AND APPLY NOW!
scan to visit their profile

Accepting applications from* B C E H I L M P S T

Types of opportunities `Graduate jobs` `Internships`

Location of opportunities ⦿ Melbourne, Sydney, Canberra, Brisbane, Perth, Darwin

WHAT IT'S LIKE?

Sally Higgins
Consultant

Consulting has given me the opportunity to work on diverse and interesting projects that I would have never imagined for myself... I also love the flexibility of self-management as a consultant at Nous. It is up to me to manage my workload across multiple projects to ensure I am meeting team and client expectations. I can shape my own work-life boundaries!

REVIEWS

☺ 'Management is highly sensitive to your physical and mental wellbeing... Flexibility is unparalleled...'

☺ 'There is an overall great culture that flows through collaborating across the business and getting to know colleagues.'

Read the full interview and more reviews at 🚀 **au.prosple.com**

#22

BDO Australia
`4.2` ★★★★☆
#4 in Accounting & advisory

LEARN MORE AND APPLY NOW!
scan to visit their profile

Accepting applications from* B C E H I L M P S

Types of opportunities `Graduate jobs` `Internships`

Location of opportunities ⦿ Perth, Sydney, Melbourne, Brisbane, Cairns, Adelaide, Hobart, Darwin

WHAT IT'S LIKE?

Keira Clark
Graduate - Tax

The culture at BDO is amazing and in my five months since starting I've felt so supported. There are a lot of opportunities for training and development - BDO puts CA master classes on, holds weekly training, and there were also grad inductions when we first started.

REVIEWS

☺ 'Flexible WFH schedule, frequent office events, excellent team culture'

☺ 'Managers are extremely approachable and accessible.'

Read the full interview and more reviews at 🚀 **au.prosple.com**

---

key for degrees where they accept applications from on page 7

#23

NSW Government
`3.9` ★★★★☆
#1 in Government & public service

Accepting applications from*	B C E H I L M P S T
Types of opportunities	Graduate jobs Internships
Location of opportunities	⦿ Sydney

WHAT IT'S LIKE?

Nicola Jones
Graduate in Insights and Industry Analysis Team

My role as a graduate has offered me a wide range of experience and opportunities to develop myself personally and professionally... There are also opportunities for me to develop my skills in engineering design including property and construction, to roads and transport, waste management and water infrastructure.

REVIEWS

☺ 'At the end of the graduate program there is a guaranteed job, however there is also the possibility of a promotion...'

☺ 'Diversity is a huge priority in the NSW government... There are proactive programs to ensure this is embodied, rather than just lip service.'

Read the full interview and more reviews at 🚀 **au.prosple.com**

#24

Mastercard Australia
`4.4` ★★★★⯪
#4 in Technology

Accepting applications from*	B C E H I L M P S T
Types of opportunities	Graduate jobs Internships
Location of opportunities	⦿ Sydney, Melbourne

WHAT IT'S LIKE?

Winnie Jiang
Associate Analyst, Business Development

The best thing about my job is that I am empowered to do work that is actually meaningful, both to Mastercard and for my personal growth.

REVIEWS

☺ 'My manager has been incredibly supportive of me... great feedback on my performance and we check in weekly.'

☺ 'At the end of the program we will go through an interview process to be moved up within our teams.'

Read the full interview and more reviews at 🚀 **au.prosple.com**

---

*key for degrees where they accept applications from on page 7

#25

Quantium
4.4 ★★★★☆
#5 in Technology

Accepting applications from*	B E I S
Types of opportunities	Graduate jobs Internships
Location of opportunities	⊚ Sydney, Melbourne, Canberra, work from home

WHAT IT'S LIKE?

Jason Khu
Graduate Data Analyst

Quantium has a unique, relaxed culture with no strict hierarchy, which fosters a friendly and collaborative environment.

REVIEWS

☺ 'Extremely flexible, depends on team. I come in most days but we have team members who are functionally 100% remote.'

☺ 'Managers are very accessible and provide a lot of support and guidance.'

Read the full interview and more reviews at 🚀 au.prosple.com

#26

Telstra
4.0 ★★★★☆
#6 in Technology

Accepting applications from*	B C E H I L M P S T
Types of opportunities	Graduate jobs Internships
Location of opportunities	⊚ Australia wide

WHAT IT'S LIKE?

Kyah Burke
e-Commerce Specialist

As a graduate, I have been able to gain experience by working in a range of different teams and on different projects. I have also been given the opportunity to expand my technical knowledge, which I am very grateful for and I know will help my career.

REVIEWS

☺ 'They (my managers) look out for my needs and provide me with lots of information. They are good mentors as well.'

☺ 'The culture and people provide support for personal and professional development. Flexible working arrangements and flexible hours.'

Read the full interview and more reviews at 🚀 au.prosple.com

*key for degrees where they accept applications from on page 7

#27 Grant Thornton

4.1 ★★★★☆
#5 in Accounting & advisory

Accepting applications from* B I L

Types of opportunities Graduate jobs Internships

Location of opportunities ◉ Sydney, Melbourne, Brisbane, Adelaide, Cairns, Perth

WHAT IT'S LIKE?

Emma Zeibari
Audit and Assurance Associate

Every day is different, as you meet new people and get to travel to new locations. This means we get to check out some great coffee shops and food locations before we start work or during our lunch breaks! You also get to change teams for every client, so you're constantly working with different people on every job and this helps to get to know more people in your service line.

REVIEWS

☺ 'Flexibility, quality of work and autonomy. I am provided with challenges whenever requested and excellent learning opportunities.'

☺ 'The people I have worked with and experiences provided are both enriching, contributes to personal and professional growth.'

Read the full interview and more reviews at 🚀 **au.prosple.com**

#28 Jacobs Australia

4.1 ★★★★☆
#4 in Engineering consulting

Accepting applications from* B C E H I L M P S T

Types of opportunities Graduate jobs Internships

Location of opportunities ◉ Sydney, Newcastle, Melbourne, Tatura, Hobart, Adelaide, Perth, Darwin, Cairns, Townsville, Brisbane, Auckland, Christchurch, Wellington

WHAT IT'S LIKE?

Nick Trevisiol
Graduate Project Manager

I feel like I'm surrounded by colleagues and resources that will influence and motivate me to grow, not only with my career but as a person. With the mentorship from senior leaders within our company, it made the transition for Grads like myself a lot less stressful.

REVIEWS

☺ 'The company is very flexible with when and where the hours are worked.'

☺ 'Solid opportunities to tailor your work to your career interests and aspirations.'

Read the full interview and more reviews at 🚀 **au.prosple.com**

key for degrees where they accept applications from on page 7

#29 Jarden

JARDEN

4.8 ★★★★★

#4 in Banking & financial services

Accepting applications from*   B   E   H   I   L   M   S

Types of opportunities   Graduate jobs   Internships

Location of opportunities   ⊙ Sydney, Melbourne

WHAT IT'S LIKE?

Kristina Lane
Investment Banking Analyst

What drew me to Jarden was its remarkable people-centric approach. The senior members of the organization possess an exceptional hands-on mentality when it comes to nurturing the personal and professional growth of their junior counterparts.

REVIEWS

☺ 'Good pay with great bonus potential.'

☺ 'My managers are great mentors and help me feel heard within the business.'

Read the full interview and more reviews at 🚀 **au.prosple.com**

#30 RACV

RACV

4.3 ★★★★☆

#5 in Banking & financial services

Accepting applications from*   B   C   E   H   I   L   M   P   S   T

Types of opportunities   Graduate jobs

Location of opportunities   ⊙ Melbourne

WHAT IT'S LIKE?

Jonathan Brisbane
Graduate – Motoring Products

There is genuine care for everyone at RACV and we are actively encouraged to give back to the community through paid volunteer days, so it is really rewarding knowing that you are working for an organisation that will not only do right by its members but the wider community as well.

REVIEWS

☺ 'Managers are accommodating, and are very approachable.'

☺ 'Competitive salary for Graduate role.'

Read the full interview and more reviews at 🚀 **au.prosple.com**

key for degrees where they accept applications from on page 7

#31 Tibra Capital
4.1 ★★★★☆
#3 in Trading

Accepting applications from* B **E** I **S**

Types of opportunities Graduate jobs Internships

Location of opportunities ◉ Sydney, Wollongong, London

WHAT IT'S LIKE?

Dean Synnott
Junior Quant Trader

Tibra supports and encourages your own research of any new ideas I might have and provides the time for me to pursue it.

REVIEWS

☺ 'Solid base pay and opportunity for large bonuses...'

☺ 'Relaxed culture, flexible work hours.'

Read the full interview and more reviews at 📍 **au.prosple.com**

#32 Accenture Australia and New Zealand
3.8 ★★★★☆
#5 in Management consulting

Accepting applications from* B **C** E **H** I **L** M **P** S **T**

Types of opportunities Graduate jobs Internships

Location of opportunities ◉ Sydney, Melbourne, Brisbane, Perth, Adelaide, Canberra, Auckland, Wellington

WHAT IT'S LIKE?

Sky Srblin
Management Consulting Analyst

The best thing about my job is honestly the people and the culture at Accenture. I have the best team who are constantly supportive and encouraging. Networking and volunteering outside of my team is also fun as everyone is so genuine.

REVIEWS

☺ 'This job has enabled me to try different things and work in vastly different areas.'

☺ 'Everyone is so nice and willing to help each other out.'

Read the full interview and more reviews at 📍 **au.prosple.com**

*key for degrees where they accept applications from on page 7

#33

Department of Defence
Australian Government — Defence

4.1 ★★★★☆

#2 in Government & public service

LEARN MORE AND APPLY NOW!
scan to visit their profile

Accepting applications from* B C E H I L M P S T

Types of opportunities Graduate jobs — Internships

Location of opportunities ⊙ Adelaide, Brisbane, Canberra, Cairns, Darwin, Melbourne, Newcastle, Perth, Sydney

WHAT IT'S LIKE?

Shanae
Research and Innovation, Specialised Coatings and Corrosion Science

Through my work on various projects, the highlights have been the opportunity getting on board different Defence ships and submarines. It's been exciting to see the type of platforms we deal with, and experience the unique style of work. I've really enjoyed getting out in the field to collect data and solve challenging problems to help support the ADF.

REVIEWS

☺ 'Being able to work on matters that you simply can't get exposure to elsewhere. National security, international law and interaction with the ADF have been incredible to work on throughout my time with Defence.'

☺ 'Very flexible working arrangements and take care of you when you have medical issues, kids and anything...'

Read the full interview and more reviews at 🚀 **au.prosple.com**

#34

BAE Systems Australia
BAE SYSTEMS

3.9 ★★★★☆

#1 in Defence & aerospace

LEARN MORE AND APPLY NOW!
scan to visit their profile

Accepting applications from* B E H I L M S T

Types of opportunities Graduate jobs — Internships

Location of opportunities ⊙ Adelaide, Melbourne, Sydney, Newcastle, Canberra, Perth

WHAT IT'S LIKE?

Jonty
Graduate Mechatronic Engineer

BAE Systems has a great working culture. In terms of the work – I enjoy all of the tasks that I do. With every task I complete, I learn something new... There is no weekend work and stress levels are not excessive. I am really enjoying my job.

REVIEWS

☺ 'As a young female, I have felt very welcomed and treated fairly by all people in the company.'

☺ 'As a grad I am allowed to learn, make a few mistakes but grow & understand the ways of the company...'

Read the full interview and more reviews at 🚀 **au.prosple.com**

---

*key for degrees where they accept applications from on page 7

#35 — Westpac Group

WESTPAC GROUP

4.4 ★★★★½
#6 in Banking & financial services

Accepting applications from* B C E H I L M P S T

Types of opportunities Graduate jobs · Internships

Location of opportunities ⊙ New South Wales, Queensland, South Australia, Victoria, Western Australia

WHAT IT'S LIKE?

Maren Giesler
Brand & Marketing Graduate

The highlight of the graduate program is the grad cohort – everyone is inclusive and fun. There are lots of opportunities for you to mingle with your fellow grads, whether that be at one of the Graduate Learning Sessions or over a drink after work. You'll always have someone to talk to and to motivate you.

REVIEWS

☺ 'Good culture, flexible work environment, excellent pay.'

☺ 'The plethora of growth and development opportunities. Career development is a key focus through the program, with networking and connections developed organically as we move towards roll-off.'

Read the full interview and more reviews at 🚀 **au.prosple.com**

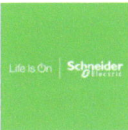

#36 — Schneider Electric Australia & New Zealand

Life Is On | Schneider Electric

4.0 ★★★★☆
#7 in Technology

Accepting applications from* B C E H I L M P S T

Types of opportunities Graduate jobs · Internships

Location of opportunities ⊙ Sydney, Melbourne, Adelaide, Perth, Brisbane, Hobart, Auckland, Wellington, Christchurch

WHAT IT'S LIKE?

Matthew Verhelst
eCommerce Content Specialist

Upon spending three months as a Summer intern, I began to pick up on the fact that Schneider practices what it preaches, in that both managers and fellow employees care for each other's well-being and career growth – in a way that does not compromise their personal lives.

REVIEWS

☺ 'Flexibility, diversity and lots of opportunities to grow your career locally and globally.'

☺ 'Everyone shows support towards each other and tries to ensure that you are feeling comfortable in your job and position.'

Read the full interview and more reviews at 🚀 **au.prosple.com**

*key for degrees where they accept applications from on page 7

#37 OPTUS

Optus
3.9 ★★★★☆
#8 in Technology

Accepting applications from*   B C E H I L M P S T

Types of opportunities   Graduate jobs

Location of opportunities   ⊙ Sydney

WHAT IT'S LIKE?

The Optus Graduate Program empowers you to craft the career you want, with resources, training & unwavering support at every step. Whether you're ready to embrace your ambitions, or looking to discover new passions, the Optus Graduate Program will help you build the career that's right for you. Our 2-year program will cycle you through a variety of different opportunities, exposing you to innovative and exciting work in every corner of the business.

REVIEWS

☺ 'We have quite a competitive salary, and higher than the industry average.'

☺ 'The people, constant support, great opportunities. A great emphasis is on being involved in various groups, activities, and events outside your day-to-day work.'

Read the full interview and more reviews at 🚀 au.prosple.com

#38 PITCHER PARTNERS

Pitcher Partners
4.2 ★★★★☆
#6 in Accounting & advisory

Accepting applications from*   B E I L

Types of opportunities   Graduate jobs   Internships

Location of opportunities   ⊙ Melbourne

WHAT IT'S LIKE?

Patricia Cattolico
Graduate Analyst

I feel like the biggest difference here is that they actually mean what they say, whereas in other companies, you could get told things, and it doesn't actually eventuate into anything. I feel like everyone's always honest and transparent about everything, which I think is super important.

REVIEWS

☺ '...they also care about your personal life as much as your work life, so they make you feel comfortable and free to talk to.'

☺ 'There is a clear progression path... there are great opportunities to accelerate your career.'

Read the full interview and more reviews at 🚀 au.prosple.com

key for degrees where they accept applications from on page 7

#39

EY Australia

3.8 ★★★★☆

#7 in Accounting & advisory

LEARN MORE AND APPLY NOW!

scan to visit their profile

Accepting applications from* B C E H I L M P S T

Types of opportunities `Graduate jobs` `Internships`

Location of opportunities ⊙ Australian Capital Territory, New South Wales, Northern Territory, Queensland, South Australia, Victoria, Western Australia

WHAT IT'S LIKE?

Isobel Bleddyn
Consultant, Strategy and Transactions

EY has so many opportunities outside of day to day work. There is volunteering with EY Ripples, sponsored further education and secondments to EY offices around the world. These opportunities create a culture where you are encouraged to develop both personally and professionally.

REVIEWS

☺ 'Empowered to have a voice no matter your rank.'

☺ 'Flexible working, diverse teams, supportive team members, wide range of work and opportunities to pursue.'

Read the full interview and more reviews at ⚲ **au.prosple.com**

#40

HERBERT SMITH FREEHILLS

Herbert Smith Freehills

4.4 ★★★★☆

#1 in Law

LEARN MORE AND APPLY NOW!

scan to visit their profile

Accepting applications from* L

Types of opportunities `Graduate jobs` `Clerkships`

Location of opportunities ⊙ Brisbane, Melbourne, Perth, Sydney

WHAT IT'S LIKE?

Siobhan Lane
Solicitor – Technology, Media and Telecommunications

All graduates at Herbert Smith Freehills are able to apply for a six-month international secondment as part of the graduate program in either your third rotation, or as an optional fourth rotation. As part of the application process, you can choose to go to Tokyo, London, Seoul, Singapore or Hong Kong...

REVIEWS

☺ 'The pay is very good... there is no feeling of competition or stress to do well during the rotations.'

☺ 'Great location, really good cafe, and building facilities.'

Read the full interview and more reviews at ⚲ **au.prosple.com**

*key for degrees where they accept applications from on page 7

#41 fuse

Fuse Recruitment

`4.3` ★★★★☆

#1 in Recruitment & HR

Accepting applications from*	B C E H I L M P S
Types of opportunities	Graduate jobs Internships
Location of opportunities	⊙ Melbourne, Brisbane, Adelaide, Parramatta

WHAT IT'S LIKE?

Amarlie Rostirolla
Recruitment Intern

I enjoy writing job advertisements as it allows me to express my creativity whilst learning more about the manufacturing industry. I also like conducting reference checks as it allows me to gain confidence talking to industry professionals, and gain insight into the manufacturing industry.

REVIEWS

🙂 'A very open and social workplace, with each day feeling as though you're going to work with your friends.'

🙂 '... very cohesive training plan in place and the team was so supportive and patient...'

Read the full interview and more reviews at 🚀 **au.prosple.com**

#42

Australian Government
Australian Security
Intelligence Organisation

Australian Security Intelligence Organisation (ASIO)

#3 in Government & public service

Accepting applications from*	B C E H I L M P S T
Types of opportunities	Graduate jobs Internships
Location of opportunities	⊙ Canberra

WHAT IT'S LIKE?

Maria
Forensic Specialist

There are a lot of career opportunities at ASIO. The organisation provides opportunities for people to move around to new areas, try new roles and find their work-life balance.

Tom
Technologist Graduate

ASIO is a great workplace because, as an Intelligence Analyst, you can move into another analytical role in another section of the Organisation every three years (if you want a change).

*key for degrees where they accept applications from on page 7

#43 Queensland Government

4.2 ★★★★☆

#4 in Government & public service

Accepting applications from*   B   C   E   H   I   L   M   P   S   T

Types of opportunities   Graduate jobs

Location of opportunities   ⊚ Queensland

WHAT IT'S LIKE?

Our graduate programs are designed to give you valuable learning and development opportunities across various agencies, focus areas and disciplines, all while making a positive impact across Queensland.

REVIEWS

☺ 'The team around you is incredibly friendly and will always take the time to explain/ introduce you to the work...'

☺ 'Flexible working has been a great perk.'

Read the full interview and more reviews at 🚀 **au.prosple.com**

#44 Rio Tinto

4.0 ★★★★☆

#2 in Mining, oil & gas

Accepting applications from*   B   E   H   I   P   S

Types of opportunities   Graduate jobs   Internships

Location of opportunities   ⊚ Multiple locations in Australia and New Zealand

WHAT IT'S LIKE?

Our Graduate and Intern Programs will provide you with opportunities to shape Rio Tinto from the inside out. For Graduates, the program is 2-years with a focus on foundational and future skills. For Interns, the program is 12-weeks across summer, with an opportunity to secure a graduate position at the end.

REVIEWS

☺ 'Pay is excellent compared to other non-mining companies. Plenty of benefits. Annual bonuses.'

☺ 'Opportunity for growth and exposure to so many different people and fields of work.'

Read the full interview and more reviews at 🚀 **au.prosple.com**

key for degrees where they accept applications from on page 7

#45

John Holland
`4.3` ★★★★☆

#1 in Construction & property services

LEARN MORE AND APPLY NOW!
scan to visit their profile

Accepting applications from*	B C E H I L M P S T
Types of opportunities	Graduate jobs Internships
Location of opportunities	⊙ Victoria, New South Wales, Queensland, Western Australia, South Australia

WHAT IT'S LIKE?

Vinh Nguyen
Rail Graduate

The rotation in projects allows you to meet new people all the time and being challenged to learn more every day.

REVIEWS

☺ '...I was pleasantly surprised that 50% of my team are women in engineering.'

☺ 'Pay is good, above average for a graduate engineer.'

Read the full interview and more reviews at 🚀 **au.prosple.com**

#46

Woodside Energy

Woodside Energy
`3.9` ★★★★☆

#3 in Mining, oil & gas

LEARN MORE AND APPLY NOW!
scan to visit their profile

Accepting applications from*	B C E H I L M P S T
Types of opportunities	Graduate jobs Internships
Location of opportunities	⊙ Perth, with some site based rotational opportunities available in Karratha

WHAT IT'S LIKE?

John Tawo
Pluto Expansion Logistics Lead

During my 3-year graduate program I worked in different teams within logistics. Working in all these different teams and with all my colleagues, leaders and mentors in the business has given me the opportunity to start building a foundation as a logistics professional.

REVIEWS

☺ 'Pay and bonuses are good.'

☺ 'Managers prioritise graduate development... very good with feedback and recognition.'

Read the full interview and more reviews at 🚀 **au.prosple.com**

---

key for degrees where they accept applications from on page 7

#47 Ashurst

Ashurst
`4.4` ★★★★☆
#2 in Law

Accepting applications from*	L
Types of opportunities	Graduate jobs Clerkships
Location of opportunities	⊙ Sydney, Melbourne, Brisbane, Canberra, Perth

WHAT IT'S LIKE?

Karen Wang
Law Graduate

The coolest thing I worked on personally was an airplane financing deal, in which I was able to work directly with a partner in my team at that time to help a company purchase an airplane… and I was able to participate in all the client calls and assist the partner directly.

REVIEWS

☺ 'Graduate pay is top of the market and highest highest-paid graduate salary in 2023.'

☺ 'Great social culture outside of work, be that exercise, after-work drinks or morning coffees.'

Read the full interview and more reviews at 🚀 **au.prosple.com**

#48 aurecon

Aurecon Australia
`4.1` ★★★★☆
#5 in Engineering consulting

Accepting applications from*	B C E H I L M P S T
Types of opportunities	Graduate jobs Internships
Location of opportunities	⊙ Adelaide, Brisbane, Cairns, Canberra, Darwin, Gladstone, Gold Coast, Mackay, Maroochydore, Melbourne, Newcastle, Perth, Sydney, Toowoomba

WHAT IT'S LIKE?

Dana Crier
Mechanical Engineer

One of the things I enjoy most about my job is working with my team and the chance to work with people who have a range of experiences and different engineering specialisations.

REVIEWS

☺ 'Great exposure to major design projects. Good team to work with. Technical training through internal knowledge share and daily works'

☺ 'Aurecon has an incredibly accommodating workplace, especially for someone with disability like me. I have found the culture to be so healthy and safe. I also love how much gender balance there is here.'

Read the full interview and more reviews at 🚀 **au.prosple.com**

key for degrees where they accept applications from on page 7

#49 VISAGIO

Visagio
`4.6` ★★★★⯪
#6 in Management consulting

Accepting applications from*   B   E   I   S

Types of opportunities   Graduate jobs   Internships

Location of opportunities   ◉ Australian Capital Territory, New South Wales, Northern Territory, Queensland, South Australia, Tasmania, Victoria, Western Australia

WHAT IT'S LIKE?

Cheng Liu
Management Consultant

Whenever I encounter a question, it is incredibly convenient to reach out to an expert within Visagio, and they are always willing to dedicate their time and expertise, allowing me to grasp the necessary knowledge and skills quickly.

REVIEWS

☺ 'Performance evaluation cycles occur every 6 months, with an opportunity for promotion.'

☺ 'The pay is higher than most companies for recent graduates.'

Read the full interview and more reviews at 🚀 **au.prosple.com**

#50 WB

William Buck
`4.3` ★★★★☆
#8 in Accounting & advisory

Accepting applications from*   B   C   L

Types of opportunities   Graduate jobs   Internships

Location of opportunities   ◉ Australia

WHAT IT'S LIKE?

Lauren Wallace
Auditor

The culture at William Buck is the main reason why I enjoy coming to work every day. It makes you feel as though you are not alone, especially when starting out as a Graduate!

REVIEWS

☺ '...clear opportunities to progress in this firm.'

☺ 'Managers are very accessible - they provide great support and are dedicated to our development.'

Read the full interview and more reviews at 🚀 **au.prosple.com**

---

key for degrees where they accept applications from on page 7

#51 — Susquehanna International Group (SIG)

4.7 ★★★★★
#4 in Trading

Accepting applications from* B C E H I L M S

Types of opportunities Graduate jobs | Internships

Location of opportunities ◉ Sydney

WHAT IT'S LIKE?

Michael Freeman
Quantitative Trader

The education and collaboration culture is great. I enjoy doing quantitative analysis and running trading tools for the team. I also enjoy the process of learning more about the markets each day.

REVIEWS

☺ 'Salary is very competitive. There are free breakfast, lunch, and insurance.'

☺ 'Loads of cooperation between teams, people are happy to help and share knowledges. I felt respected and be taken seriously by senior and managers. I do hang out with some colleagues in after hours.'

Read the full interview and more reviews at ◈ au.prosple.com

#52 — AECOM

3.8 ★★★★☆
#6 in Engineering consulting

Accepting applications from* B E I P S

Types of opportunities Graduate jobs | Internships

Location of opportunities ◉ Adelaide, Brisbane, Cairns, Canberra, Darwin, Gold Coast, Newcastle, Mackay, Maroochydore, Melbourne, Perth, Rockhampton, Sydney, Townsville

WHAT IT'S LIKE?

Kesh Preeyadarshanan
Civil Engineer

AECOM at its core is about the people, and I enjoy coming in to work and having chats with people from a variety of backgrounds and career levels, about both work and life!

REVIEWS

☺ 'I still wake up every morning excited to go into the office... No company or employer has managed to keep me on my toes for that long.'

☺ 'Extremely approachable, supportive, provide great feedback...'

Read the full interview and more reviews at ◈ au.prosple.com

key for degrees where they accept applications from on page 7

#53 — Ramsay Health Care

Ramsay Health Care
3.6 ★★★☆☆
#1 in Health

Accepting applications from* M

Types of opportunities Graduate jobs | Internships

Location of opportunities 📍 Queensland, New South Wales, South Australia, Victoria, Western Australia

WHAT IT'S LIKE?

Cynthia Lee
Registered Nurse

The biggest highlight for me would be that every and any patient can be unpredictable… It challenges me to think, respond and display my leadership skills… It is such a warming and fun environment. Everyone is supportive and can talk together about almost anything.

REVIEWS

☺ 'Flexibility with rostering and shifts, being able to maintain a work life balance.'

☺ 'The amazing support I have had from day 1 from my colleagues, the graduate coordinators and the management teams…'

Read the full interview and more reviews at 🚀 **au.prosple.com**

#54 — AngloGold Ashanti Australia

AngloGold Ashanti Australia
4.2 ★★★★☆
#4 in Mining, oil & gas

Accepting applications from* B E H I M P S

Types of opportunities Graduate jobs | Internships

Location of opportunities 📍 Western Australia

WHAT IT'S LIKE?

Russia Zeedan
Exploration Geologist

My job is unbelievably cool. I get to work hundreds of metres underground within host rocks that are 2.67 million years old! I get to see the result of mineralisation processes that formed gold with my own eyes.

REVIEWS

☺ 'The people are very supportive and willing to help/spread years of knowledge to new starters.'

☺ 'A good attitude towards making the workplace as diverse as possible. The company sees the value in being flexible to retain employees and in hiring across a diverse range of people'

Read the full interview and more reviews at 🚀 **au.prosple.com**

key for degrees where they accept applications from on page 7

#55

Unilever Australia and New Zealand

`4.3` ★★★★☆

#3 in Retail & consumer goods

LEARN MORE AND APPLY NOW!

scan to visit their profile

Accepting applications from*   B C E H I L M P S T

Types of opportunities   `Graduate jobs` `Internships`

Location of opportunities   ◉ Sydney, Auckland

WHAT IT'S LIKE?

Aanya Jain
UFLP Human Resources

I feel lucky to have regular one-on-ones with the HR director of the company, who has provided me with incredible guidance, support, and career advice throughout the programme.

REVIEWS

☺ 'Flexibility / 4-day work week.'

☺ 'Within my current role as a graduate, I have already been given numerous promotions and increased responsibility.'

Read the full interview and more reviews at ⚡ **au.prosple.com**

#56

Fujitsu

`4.6` ★★★★½

#9 in Technology

LEARN MORE AND APPLY NOW!

scan to visit their profile

Accepting applications from*   B C E H I L M P S T

Types of opportunities   `Graduate jobs`

Location of opportunities   ◉ Adelaide, Brisbane, Canberra, Melbourne, Sydney

---

WHAT IT'S LIKE?

Reinaldo Capizzi
Co Creation Analyst

You get a load of opportunities to meet different people, and a lot of them adopt a really helpful approach to aiding your learning or giving you opportunities to try something new when they learn you are a Graduate.

REVIEWS

☺ 'The company's culture is very positive. There are many opportunities within the company itself, and Fujitsu allows one to learn in different areas.'

☺ 'Good company benefits and discounts on everyday things, which is cool.'

Read the full interview and more reviews at ⚡ **au.prosple.com**

---

key for degrees where they accept applications from on page 7

#57 RSM Australia

RSM Australia
4.1 ★★★★☆
#9 in Accounting & advisory

Accepting applications from* B E H I L M S

Types of opportunities Graduate jobs | Internships

Location of opportunities ⦿ Multiple locations in Australia

WHAT IT'S LIKE?

Rupert Middleton
Graduate

Through my short time at RSM, I've worked on clients across a broad range of industries... Not only this, audit is a very team-oriented job and it is very rare for you to be working on a client by yourself. This gives you an opportunity to develop your soft skills like teamwork, communication and presentation.

REVIEWS

☺ 'A clear upward career path is laid out, generally a grad for 1 year as the grad program runs for 1 year...'

☺ 'Good work-life balance, a clear career path, a good team, good leadership, lots of events...'

Read the full interview and more reviews at ⚲ **au.prosple.com**

#58 Shell

Shell
4.8 ★★★★★
#5 in Mining, oil & gas

Accepting applications from* B E I L M S

Types of opportunities Graduate jobs | Internships

Location of opportunities ⦿ Brisbane, Gladstone, Perth, Chinchilla

WHAT IT'S LIKE?

Joanna Wong
Process Technical Safety Engineer

The graduate programme is three years long and, during this time, I know I will get a well-rounded view of all the assets and the technical disciplines in this large organisation. My peers who have joined the programme speak very highly of it. The opportunity to travel for work is also attractive to me.

REVIEWS

☺ 'The office culture is very good and the graduate cohort is extremely close.'

☺ 'Much higher pay than I had hoped/expected, with performance bonuses to sweeten the deal.'

Read the full interview and more reviews at ⚲ **au.prosple.com**

key for degrees where they accept applications from on page 7

#59

Monadelphous
4.1 ★★★★☆
#2 in Construction & property services

LEARN MORE AND APPLY NOW!
scan to visit their profile

Accepting applications from*   B   E   P   S

Types of opportunities   Graduate jobs   Internships

Location of opportunities   ◎ Brisbane, Perth

WHAT IT'S LIKE?

Mario Du Plessis
Construction Management Graduate

What I enjoy most about my job is the people I get to work with. Working collaboratively on projects and the sense of comradery when completing projects is extremely fulfilling. With the Monadelphous culture, support and encouragement I believe anyone with the right attitude and interest will be able to be successful in my role at Monadelphous.

REVIEWS

☺ 'The culture and people are incredibly supportive, willing to teach you anything, and very inclusive.'

☺ 'I am very happy with my pay; the food allowance and site uplift for being FIFO are also good.'

Read the full interview and more reviews at 🚀 **au.prosple.com**

#60

Nova Systems
3.8 ★★★★☆
#2 in Defence & aerospace

LEARN MORE AND APPLY NOW!
scan to visit their profile

Accepting applications from*   B   C   E   I   M   S

Types of opportunities   Graduate jobs   Internships

Location of opportunities   ◎ Adelaide

WHAT IT'S LIKE?

Chante Swart
Systems Engineer

I really love the social and people aspect of Nova. So not only has it been amazing that I could join the social committee and help run social and charitable events such as the biggest morning tea bake-off, but I also got the opportunity to help with the work experience and graduate program.

REVIEWS

☺ 'Everyone is welcoming and inclusive, and I have formed strong friendships with other grads.'

☺ 'They (my managers) have supported me and assisted with formulating my career goals and helping me achieve them.'

Read the full interview and more reviews at 🚀 **au.prosple.com**

key for degrees where they accept applications from on page 7

#61  Boeing
4.3 ★★★★☆
#3 in Defence & aerospace

LEARN MORE AND APPLY NOW!
scan to visit their profile

Accepting applications from* B E I L S

Types of opportunities Graduate jobs Internships

Location of opportunities ⊙ Australian Capital Territory, New South Wales, Northern Territory, Queensland, South Australia, Victoria, Western Australia

WHAT IT'S LIKE?

Alexander Bowen-Rotsaert
Systems Engineer

There's tremendous scope to work on interesting and challenging development projects, with very talented people, and on some pretty amazing technology and equipment.

REVIEWS

☺ 'Great office environment, company actively supports and encourages good work-life balance.'

☺ 'They are very flexible around hours including start times, finish times, and lunch break times/lengths.'

Read the full interview and more reviews at 🚀 **au.prosple.com**

#62  Australian Taxation Office (ATO)
4.2 ★★★★☆
#5 in Government & public service

LEARN MORE AND APPLY NOW!
scan to visit their profile

Accepting applications from* B C E H I L M P S T

Types of opportunities Graduate jobs

Location of opportunities ⊙ Adelaide, Albury, Brisbane, Canberra, Geelong, Gosford, Hobart, Melbourne, Newcastle, Perth, Sydney, Townsville, Wollongong

WHAT IT'S LIKE?

Zoe Penson
Graduate Officer

The thing I love most about ATO is that the work we do has real-world implications and impact on the community. During my Superannuation and Employer Obligations rotation, I handled cases of employers not paying superannuation to their employees. I had the opportunity to speak to the employees and hear their stories firsthand and achieve meaningful results for them. It was very rewarding to help taxpayers and ensure businesses were meeting their obligations.

*key for degrees where they accept applications from on page 7

REVIEWS

☺ 'The Graduate Program also offers mentorship when doing assessments which creates further networks of support.'

☺ 'I see many opportunities for career progression. My current leadership supports me applying for these opportunities.'

Read the full interview and more reviews at 🚀 **au.prosple.com**

#63

CSIRO
4.4 ★★★★½
#1 in R&D and manufacturing

LEARN MORE AND APPLY NOW!
scan to visit their profile

Accepting applications from* B C E H I L M P S T

Types of opportunities Graduate jobs Internships

Location of opportunities ⊙ Australian Capital Territory, New South Wales, Northern Territory, Queensland, South Australia, Tasmania, Victoria, Western Australia

WHAT IT'S LIKE?

Dr Katie Hillyer
CSIRO Early Research Career (CERC) Postdoctoral Fellow

Team CSIRO is also generally a great place to work, and I feel genuinely proud have been a part of Australia's national science agency and what we are achieving.

REVIEWS

☺ 'CSIRO is very flexible with work hours. They want their staff to have a good work/life balance.'

☺ 'Everyone is approachable and helpful to any questions asked, and very accepting.'

Read the full interview and more reviews at 🚀 **au.prosple.com**

#64

DXC Technology
3.3 ★★★☆☆
#10 in Technology

LEARN MORE AND APPLY NOW!
scan to visit their profile

Accepting applications from* B C E H I L M P S T

Types of opportunities Graduate jobs

Location of opportunities ⊙ Australian Capital Territory, New South Wales, Northern Territory, Queensland, South Australia, Tasmania, Victoria, Western Australia

WHAT IT'S LIKE?

James Lam
Associate Business Consultant

One of the best parts about my job is being able to interact with and learn from such great minds. Being in an environment where we are encouraged to reach out to share ideas and thoughts is awesome.

REVIEWS

☺ 'Opportunities to work with large companies in the technology field.'

☺ 'Having a large enough graduate cohort to be a part of provides me with the opportunity to ask questions of other young people within the organisation'

Read the full interview and more reviews at 🚀 **au.prosple.com**

key for degrees where they accept applications from on page 7

#65 Honeywell

Honeywell
`4.2` ★★★★☆
#11 in Technology

Accepting applications from*	B C E H I S
Types of opportunities	Graduate jobs Internships
Location of opportunities	⊙ Australian Capital Territory, New South Wales, Queensland, Tasmania, Victoria, Western Australia, Auckland

WHAT IT'S LIKE?

Riley Toi
Graduate Engineer

I am fortunate that I get to work in multiple disciplines throughout the day. Whether the project is in building control, security or smart analytics, my expertise is needed to help the customer make crucial decisions that benefit their companies or tenants.

REVIEWS

☺ 'Honeywell is very firm on inclusivity for women and upholds fantastic ethics and values.'

☺ 'Pay is great, pay rise will depend on performance even for graduates, you can get a pay rise if you over perform.'

Read the full interview and more reviews at 🚀 **au.prosple.com**

#66 SLB

SLB
`3.9` ★★★★☆
#12 in Technology

Accepting applications from*	E I S T
Types of opportunities	Graduate jobs Internships
Location of opportunities	⊙ Queensland, South Australia, Western Australia, Global

WHAT IT'S LIKE?

Sarah Jayne-Robinson
Drilling Fluids Specialist

I really like that Schlumberger invests so much time and money in training and that you don't really need to have a background knowledge in the subject before you come to the technical school.

REVIEWS

☺ 'The growth expectations of everyone in their own careers lead to knowledge sharing and cheering for coworker achievements.'

☺ 'Whether they are cross-geographies or functions, you can tailor your career to fit your needs.'

Read the full interview and more reviews at 🚀 **au.prosple.com**

key for degrees where they accept applications from on page 7

#67

Dulux Group
`4.3` ★★★★☆

#4 in Retail & consumer goods

LEARN MORE AND APPLY NOW!

scan to visit their profile

Accepting applications from* B C E H I L M P S T

Types of opportunities Graduate jobs

Location of opportunities ⊙ New South Wales, Queensland, Victoria, South Australia, Western Australia

WHAT IT'S LIKE?

Eleanor Wilcock
Marketing Coordinator

DuluxGroup also has a great culture, and there is always something exciting or different happening – be it an interstate conference, a morning tea with the Clayton site, or a learning workshop.

REVIEWS

☺ 'Flexibility of Work From Anywhere. I'm able to come to the office 2 - 3 days a week and WFH for the rest!'

☺ 'Work life balance - everyone is respectful of differing working hours and will make sure team members aren't logging off too late.'

Read the full interview and more reviews at 🚀 **au.prosple.com**

#68

Protiviti
`3.6` ★★★⯪☆

#7 in Management consulting

LEARN MORE AND APPLY NOW!

scan to visit their profile

Accepting applications from* B C E H I L M P S T

Types of opportunities Graduate jobs

Location of opportunities ⊙ Brisbane, Canberra, Melbourne, Sydney

WHAT IT'S LIKE?

Brendon Kim
Senior Consultant

With our flat structure, graduates work directly with our directors and partners to deliver client work, giving us the perfect opportunity to learn from the best of the best. There's enough trust in the company for you to work with clients directly including their management team.

REVIEWS

☺ 'The people and the culture are great. The leadership team are approachable.'

☺ 'Managers have been more than happy to help when I have reached out. Feedback on all projects has been extremely helpful in improving my weaknesses.'

Read the full interview and more reviews at 🚀 **au.prosple.com**

*key for degrees where they accept applications from on page 7

#69 ⬡ Stantec

Stantec Australia
`4.1` ★★★★☆
#7 in Engineering consulting

Accepting applications from*	B E I P S
Types of opportunities	Graduate jobs · Internships
Location of opportunities	⊙ Australia wide

WHAT IT'S LIKE?

Elise Hor
Graduate Mechanical Engineer

Aside from working with extraordinary people, I think being able to see your own designs come to life is very enjoyable... Sharing ideas and knowledge between clients, architects, builders, and other consultants to come together and create a smart building that is not only liveable but sustainable and aesthetic...

REVIEWS

☺ 'Understanding leaders which support the needs of different individuals - either from arranging flexible work arrangements, giving opportunities to learn new things and even try work of other teams.'

☺ 'Very helpful colleagues, plenty of events to learn and relax at the office and outside of office.'

Read the full interview and more reviews at 🚀 **au.prosple.com**

#70 **KraftHeinz**

Kraft Heinz Company
`4.2` ★★★★☆
#5 in Retail & consumer goods

Accepting applications from*	B C E H I L S
Types of opportunities	Graduate jobs
Location of opportunities	⊙ Melbourne, Seven Hills, Northgate

WHAT IT'S LIKE?

Alyssia Santilli
R&D Technologist

Being a foodie lover, it was a given to apply for an FMCG company! So many tastings! There is not a week that goes by where a tasting isn't conducted - this could be tasting a competitor product, new product development in the market, bench prototypes, production trials, all the way through to shelf life evaluations postlaunch.

REVIEWS

☺ 'People are so friendly & helpful inside of work & extremely social outside of it.'

☺ 'Part of the culture is meritocracy, so rewarding people for hard work & this can be in the form of a promotion. As it is a global company there are also opportunities outside your country of origin.'

Read the full interview and more reviews at 🚀 **au.prosple.com**

*key for degrees where they accept applications from on page 7

#71

SW Accountants & Advisors
4.3 ★★★★☆
#10 in Accounting & advisory

Accepting applications from*   B E I L S

Types of opportunities   Graduate jobs   Internships

Location of opportunities   ⊙ Sydney, Brisbane, Melbourne, Perth

WHAT IT'S LIKE?

Laura Nield
Intermediate Consultant

Juggling full-time work and studies can be overwhelming. However, SW provides an exceptional support network that extends beyond the CA program, covering day-to-day responsibilities within the role. This ensures that, even during the most demanding times, you never feel like you're navigating challenges alone.

REVIEWS

☺ '...enjoyable working environment that makes me want to come into the office, but support working from home and flexible hours.'

☺ 'SW has a very supportive and collaborative work culture. As a grad, I was well looked after.'

Read the full interview and more reviews at 🚀 **au.prosple.com**

#72

TAL Australia
4.4 ★★★★☆
#7 in Banking & financial services

Accepting applications from*   B E H I L M S

Types of opportunities   Graduate jobs   Internships

Location of opportunities   ⊙ Sydney

WHAT IT'S LIKE?

Alanah Hall
Claims Consultant

Working in the Claims team at TAL is a very rewarding job. We spend each and every day assisting customers throughout what is usually a very difficult time in their lives. You learn to be a very good listener and communicator and to see things from different perspectives.

REVIEWS

☺ 'We can come into the office every day if we want to, but most people do 2-3 days in the office and 2 from home.'

☺ 'Great people, low stress, interesting and varied work, opportunities to grow, and a sense of purpose.'

Read the full interview and more reviews at 🚀 **au.prosple.com**

---

*key for degrees where they accept applications from on page 7

#73 VivCourt Trading

VIVCOURT TRADING

4.7 ★★★★★

#5 in Trading

Accepting applications from*	E I S
Types of opportunities	Graduate jobs Internships
Location of opportunities	⊙ Sydney, work from home

WHAT IT'S LIKE?

Michael Rodwell
Delta Trader

There are many aspects of my work that I love! I enjoy the intellectual challenge and the technical conversations and projects that my team can engage with. It's also very rewarding to have a tight feedback loop from the work you do and the success you can achieve.

REVIEWS

☺ 'The base pay and bonuses are competitive in the industry.'

☺ 'No dress codes. Brilliant location in Paddington and colourful office.'

Read the full interview and more reviews at 🚀 **au.prosple.com**

#74 Akuna Capital

akuna

4.4 ★★★★☆

#6 in Trading

Accepting applications from*	B E I S T
Types of opportunities	Graduate jobs Internships
Location of opportunities	⊙ Sydney

WHAT IT'S LIKE?

Lumina
Quantitative Development Intern

The main technical skills you need to succeed as a quantitative developer is a combination of mathematical and programming expertise, but most importantly you must be a strong problem solver.

REVIEWS

☺ 'Good racial diversity... we're seeing the proportion of women increase in the office.'

☺ 'Pay and bonuses are on the very top end of potential graduate compensation, very attractive.'

Read the full interview and more reviews at 🚀 **au.prosple.com**

---

*key for degrees where they accept applications from on page 7

#75

Allens

`4.5` ★★★★⯪

#3 in Law

Accepting applications from* `L`

Types of opportunities `Graduate jobs` `Clerkships`

Location of opportunities ⊙ Sydney, Melbourne, Brisbane, Perth

WHAT IT'S LIKE?

Emma Cockburn
Law Graduate

It's exciting to work in teams of highly experienced lawyers – I am constantly impressed by the mentorship and guidance they offer!

REVIEWS

☺ 'The work culture is amazing. There is good support for graduates and lots of good stretch opportunities for young lawyers.'

☺ 'Fantastic training and mentorships, as long as you are willing to learn and engage.'

Read the full interview and more reviews at 🚀 **au.prosple.com**

#76

Transgrid

`4.3` ★★★★☆

#1 in Energy & utilities

Accepting applications from* `B` `C` `E` `H` `I` `L` `M` `P` `S`

Types of opportunities `Graduate jobs` `Internships`

Location of opportunities ⊙ New South Wales

WHAT IT'S LIKE?

Mohammed Zaid Khan
Project Management Graduate

If projects is your career goals, I would be surprised if any other organisation would be providing similar opportunities at such an early stage in your career and I truly believe that the TransGrid graduate program sets you up to be an experienced project manager.

REVIEWS

☺ 'For my experience level, my pay is very good. My opportunities for moving up are also very good.'

☺ 'There are neurodivergent individuals within the business who receive appropriate accommodations and can be their best selves at the workplace because of this.'

Read the full interview and more reviews at 🚀 **au.prosple.com**

key for degrees where they accept applications from on page 7

#77

Dolby Australia
4.5 ★★★★½
#13 in Technology

Accepting applications from*	C E I
Types of opportunities	Graduate jobs Internships
Location of opportunities	⊙ Sydney

WHAT IT'S LIKE?

Dylan Harper-Harris
Software Engineer

I love that I am able to design algorithms and train neural networks in a research context, on audio, and within Australia. Also, we have the coolest labs! And movie days too!

REVIEWS

☺ 'Flexible working hours with the ability to choose to work in office or remotely.'

☺ 'The managers are always open to feedback and treat everyone equally regardless of position.'

Read the full interview and more reviews at ⚲ **au.prosple.com**

#78

McGrathNicol
McGrathNicol
4.2 ★★★★☆
#11 in Accounting & advisory

Accepting applications from*	B C E H I L S
Types of opportunities	Graduate jobs Internships
Location of opportunities	⊙ Brisbane, Canberra, Melbourne Perth, Sydney

WHAT IT'S LIKE?

Natalie Thompson
Analyst, Cyber

My largest limitation is what I don't know, but the fact is that employees are more than happy to share their knowledge. Over the past 10 months, I have learnt so much because others are willing to share what they know.

REVIEWS

☺ 'People are very friendly and easy-going. Senior management is always happy to help assist and guide graduates.'

☺ 'The firm is highly flexible with work hours.'

Read the full interview and more reviews at ⚲ **au.prosple.com**

---

key for degrees where they accept applications from on page 7

#79

Department of the Prime Minister and Cabinet (PM&C)

`4.2` ★★★★☆

#6 in Government & public service

Accepting applications from*	B C E H I L M P S T
Types of opportunities	Graduate jobs Internships
Location of opportunities	⦿ Canberra

WHAT IT'S LIKE?

Edwin Anderson
Graduate

The best part of the graduate year at PM&C is the rotations because they allow you to try out almost anywhere within PM&C. Other grads are working in everything from behavioral economics, the Office for Women, to social policy including education, immigration, and infrastructure.

REVIEWS

☺ 'I have the flexibility to work from home, start early and finish early, or start later and finish later.'

☺ 'PM&C has a very flat hierarchy. Often, our senior officers will sit at desks on the floor with us instead of in offices, and as a junior in the organisation I have a significant amount of face-time with my seniors. The organisation is extremely social and organise events at team, branch, and division levels.'

Read the full interview and more reviews at 🚀 **au.prosple.com**

#80

Australian Energy Market Operator (AEMO)

`4.4` ★★★★½

#2 in Energy & utilities

Accepting applications from*	B E I S
Types of opportunities	Graduate jobs Internships
Location of opportunities	⦿ Melbourne, Sydney, Norwest, Brisbane, Perth, Adelaide

WHAT IT'S LIKE?

As the nation's independent market operator, we offer all graduates an unparalleled experience. This means that you will have the opportunity to advance your career across a wide range of fields, interact with some of the brightest minds in the sector, and immediately contribute to our rapidly evolving industry.

REVIEWS

☺ 'AEMO is a very inclusive workforce, primarily driven by the individuals who work here being open-minded and respectful.'

☺ 'The once-a-year company-performance based bonus is generous and a great perk of AEMO. Salary is high for a graduate-level employee.'

Read the full interview and more reviews at 🚀 **au.prosple.com**

key for degrees where they accept applications from on page 7

#81 Bank of Queensland (BOQ)

4.2 ★★★★☆

#8 in Banking & financial services

LEARN MORE AND APPLY NOW!
scan to visit their profile

Accepting applications from* B C E H I L M P S

Types of opportunities Graduate jobs Internships

Location of opportunities ⊙ Brisbane, Sydney, Melbourne

WHAT IT'S LIKE?

Phil

BOQ runs many social events to encourage us to build relationships with people outside of our immediate teams. My favourite so far was trivia night where I was able to enjoy getting to know colleagues from other departments over pizza and drinks.

REVIEWS

☺ 'Recruitment ensures the team is an eclectic mix of people, from different racial and gender identities. It is very progressive with respect to diversity.'

☺ 'They partner with Sonder for Health for employees, Orange Sky and the Mother's Day Classic to raise money and awareness.'

Read the full interview and more reviews at 🚀 **au.prosple.com**

#82 Mineral Resources

4.3 ★★★★☆

#6 in Mining, oil & gas

LEARN MORE AND APPLY NOW!
scan to visit their profile

Accepting applications from* B C E H I L M P S

Types of opportunities Graduate jobs Internships

Location of opportunities ⊙ Western Australia

WHAT IT'S LIKE?

Merryln Mpofu
Graduate Exploration Geologist

The coolest thing about my job is that it's dynamic, I get to work at different sites every couple of months. I love the variety it's the spice of life therefore I'm always more than happy to go to new locations and learn more interesting facts about that area.

REVIEWS

☺ 'There is no sense of a 'hierarchy' and business leaders (including General Managers) are willing to socialise with anyone, regardless of their position or title.'

☺ 'Each day presents new lessons and challenges, I constantly feel like I am learning and developing.'

Read the full interview and more reviews at 🚀 **au.prosple.com**

*key for degrees where they accept applications from on page 7

#83

Lockheed Martin

4.0 ★★★★☆

#4 in Defence & aerospace

Accepting applications from*   B E H I L S T

Types of opportunities   Graduate jobs   Internships

Location of opportunities   ◉ Adelaide, Canberra

WHAT IT'S LIKE?

Josephine Delore
Hardware Engineer

My favourite thing about my job is delivering the final product to the customer at the end of a project. There is a lot of time and effort that goes into getting a product from initial design to manufacturing. It is very satisfying to see something you worked hard on being used in real life.

REVIEWS

🙂 'Pay is very competitive for a graduate salary.'

🙂 'I was expecting defence to be all dark rooms and no windows. This isn't the case at all, there's lots of plants that are watered regularly, as well as standing desks throughout. Some offices have lots of parking and dress code ranges from smart all the way down to semi-casual, depending on the stakeholders in the office at the time.'

Read the full interview and more reviews at 🚀 **au.prosple.com**

#84

acciona

ACCIONA Australia and New Zealand

4.2 ★★★★☆

#3 in Construction & property services

Accepting applications from*   B C E H I L M P S

Types of opportunities   Graduate jobs

Location of opportunities   ◉ Queensland, New South Wales, Victoria, South Australia, Western Australia, New Zealand

WHAT IT'S LIKE?

Lauryn Neto
Human Resources Graduate

I am also able to work with people like Emma Hassett who continues to drive change in the diversity and inclusion space within the construction industry particularly around encouraging more females to enter the industry.

REVIEWS

🙂 'My pay is more than I expected when entering the industry at a graduate level.'

🙂 'I have found the company to be extremely flexible with individual needs. Management is very understanding and allows a great workaround with WFH and also does not need to go beyond set hours.'

Read the full interview and more reviews at 🚀 **au.prosple.com**

*key for degrees where they accept applications from on page 7

#85 — Safe Work Australia

4.4 ★★★★☆

#7 in Government & public service

Accepting applications from* B C E H I L M P S

Types of opportunities Graduate jobs

Location of opportunities ⊙ Canberra

WHAT IT'S LIKE?

Kim Đinh
Graduate

What I love most is the team I am currently in at SWA, the High Risk Work and Industries Policy Section. This team develops and evaluates policy in relation to all things high risk-work related... I think it is a fun and dynamic team with team members who always make the most of the interesting and meaningful work.

REVIEWS

🙂 'All of the supervisors I have had during my graduate rotation have been supportive to work with.'

🙂 'The culture is close knit and you feel supported.'

Read the full interview and more reviews at 🚀 **au.prosple.com**

#86 — Department of Energy, Environment and Climate Action (DEECA)

4.4 ★★★★☆

#8 in Government & public service

Accepting applications from* B E H I M P S

Types of opportunities Graduate jobs

Location of opportunities ⊙ Melbourne, regional Victoria

WHAT IT'S LIKE?

Gracie Doherty
Graduate Environment & Sustainability Officer

The coolest thing about my role has been the opportunities I've had to get out in the field and work with critically endangered species, such as the Helmeted Honeyeaters. I've seen parts of the landscape I don't think I would have the opportunity to see otherwise and met some amazing people doing it!

REVIEWS

🙂 'Good flexibility and work/life balance. Good people and well-being is valued.'

🙂 'Incredible perks for L&D and guaranteed employment. Flexible work, moving expenses, Grad connections (a HUGE support network very early in your career), training & L&D, multiple roles to test what you like and what you don't.'

Read the full interview and more reviews at 🚀 **au.prosple.com**

*key for degrees where they accept applications from on page 7

#87

NORTHROP

Northrop Consulting Engineers
4.5 ★★★★½
#8 in Engineering consulting

Accepting applications from*   E   P   T

Types of opportunities   Graduate jobs   Internships

Location of opportunities   ⊙ Victoria, New South Wales, Queensland

WHAT IT'S LIKE?

We're inclusive and we're diverse. We want everyone who joins us to fulfil their potential, and we help, guide and sometimes push each other to achieve exactly that. We've got each other's backs, and everyone is comfortable and happy being themselves. Northrop is a home for high performers, but there's no pretence and little politics. We engage with each other and do great work together.

REVIEWS

☺ 'Flexibility with working conditions. Can have a mix between remote and in office development.'

☺ 'Managers are very accessible throughout the day and always willing to talk to you about project issues or questions. Regular mentor/manager catch ups are done to ensure there is a chance for feedback and communication.'

Read the full interview and more reviews at 🚀 **au.prosple.com**

#88

xero

Xero Australia
4.1 ★★★★☆
#14 in Technology

Accepting applications from*   B   C   E   H   I   L   M   P   S   T

Types of opportunities   Graduate jobs   Internships

Location of opportunities   ⊙ Melbourne, Canberra

WHAT IT'S LIKE?

Sabrina Swatee
Developer

What drives me is growth. Xero offers plenty opportunities to expand my skill set. This is what I love most about my job. I am not only developing the core technical skills, but non-technical as well... Through organised family coding day, career days, voluntary services, I also get to play my part in building the community besides building myself.

REVIEWS

☺ 'Culture -- work-from-home policy, generous well-being leave, friendly and interesting people.'

☺ 'At the completion of the grad year, we get promoted and a blanket salary increase.'

Read the full interview and more reviews at 🚀 **au.prosple.com**

*key for degrees where they accept applications from on page 7

#89 ◤leidos — Leidos Australia

4.1 ★★★★☆

#5 in Defence & aerospace

Accepting applications from*	B C E H I L S T
Types of opportunities	Graduate jobs · Internships
Location of opportunities	◉ Melbourne, Canberra

WHAT IT'S LIKE?

Talia Zidar
Graduate Cyber Analyst

There is always someone to talk to and ask for feedback without fear. I have access to a buddy, mentor, People Leader, a talented team of colleagues, and a wonderful graduate cohort. Leidos and the Early Careers team have built an environment that values both your well-being and career growth. I feel so supported in this role.

REVIEWS

☺ 'Managers are consistently approachable and readily available for discussions whenever needed.'

☺ 'The opportunities to have pay reviews and performance reviews are abundant and allow for many opportunities to have pay increases.'

Read the full interview and more reviews at 🚀 **au.prosple.com**

#90 tcs TATA CONSULTANCY SERVICES — Tata Consultancy Services Australia and New Zealand

4.2 ★★★★☆

#8 in Management consulting

Accepting applications from*	B E I
Types of opportunities	Graduate jobs · Internships
Location of opportunities	◉ New South Wales, Victoria, New Zealand

WHAT IT'S LIKE?

Tina Wu
Graduate

Being able to work for TCS allows me to have a better understanding of how technology is shaping the world and the extent in which information technology can assist businesses and large corporations in achieving their goals.

REVIEWS

☺ 'Managers are great at TCS they can do many things to help support you as well as upskill you for the future.'

☺ 'Outside of work, we graduates have also organised dinners to catch-up with each other.'

Read the full interview and more reviews at 🚀 **au.prosple.com**

---

key for degrees where they accept applications from on page 7

#91

South32
`4.2` ★★★★☆
#7 in Mining, oil & gas

Accepting applications from* B E I M S

Types of opportunities Graduate jobs Internships

Location of opportunities ⊙ New South Wales, Queensland, Western Australia, Northern Territory

WHAT IT'S LIKE?

Mirabelle Molukun
Graduate Mining Engineer

Being a graduate, I have a lot of flexibility to move around and work in different departments, even for a short time just to get the exposure.

REVIEWS

☺ 'Safety is their number one priority as described in break through #1 (Everyone goes home safe). They also offer flexible working hours.'

☺ 'South32 is focused on promoting diversity with respect to women, ethnic minorities and the LGBT community.'

Read the full interview and more reviews at 🚀 **au.prosple.com**

#92

Department of Health and Aged Care
`4.2` ★★★★☆
#9 in Government & public service

*Australian Government
Department of Health
and Aged Care*

Accepting applications from* B C E H I L M P S T

Types of opportunities Graduate jobs Internships

Location of opportunities ⊙ Canberra

WHAT IT'S LIKE?

Victoria Marriott
Graduate

The Grad Program for me was a fantastic opportunity to learn, grow and challenge myself in a supportive environment. I learnt quickly that most people in the Department are willing to help you out, whether it is assisting to coordinate input or simply how to get from Sirius North to Sirius South.

REVIEWS

☺ 'We have lots of diversity training opportunities and staff networks that do incredible work for women, ethnic minorities, the LGBTQI+ community, Indigenous staff and more.'

☺ 'Overall great workplace culture, stimulating and dynamic role, and encouragement to move around the agency and experience different work areas.'

Read the full interview and more reviews at 🚀 **au.prosple.com**

key for degrees where they accept applications from on page 7

#93

nbn

`4.2` ★★★★☆

#15 in Technology

Accepting applications from*	B C E H I L M P S T
Types of opportunities	Graduate jobs
Location of opportunities	◉ Sydney, Melbourne

WHAT IT'S LIKE?

Paul Tan
Graduate

The graduate program offers a large support system and it has been great having people who really care about your future give advice and guidance.

REVIEWS

☺ 'Very friendly and laid-back culture with flexible working arrangements.'

☺ 'Great starting pay for a graduate which was adjusted with inflation. The company provides a wide range of health benefits. Whether you require physical or mental health assistance, nbn has great benefits to help you maintain and help your health.'

Read the full interview and more reviews at ◤ **au.prosple.com**

#94

Rheinmetall

`4.4` ★★★★☆

#6 in Defence & aerospace

Accepting applications from*	B E I
Types of opportunities	Graduate jobs Internships
Location of opportunities	◉ Brisbane, Melbourne, Adelaide

WHAT IT'S LIKE?

Hunter Conochie
Graduate Software Engineer

You can set your own pace being a graduate at Rheinmetall. RDA is happy for you to just learn and take things in and partner with more senior engineers if that is what you want to do.

REVIEWS

☺ 'The company is super flexible with hours, as long as the work is done, and attend required meetings, can work whatever hours to make up the total hours for the working week.'

☺ 'I am working on exciting projects and I feel I am having an impact on the work I am doing.'

Read the full interview and more reviews at ◤ **au.prosple.com**

*key for degrees where they accept applications from on page 7

#95

Victorian Government

`3.8` ★★★★☆

#10 Government & public service

LEARN MORE AND APPLY NOW!
———
scan to visit their profile

Accepting applications from*	B C E H I L M P S T
Types of opportunities	Graduate jobs
Location of opportunities	⊙ Melbourne

WHAT IT'S LIKE?

Zack Green
Project Officer - Commission for Children and Young People (CCYP)

My anxiety about the recruitment process was alleviated when I spoke to the people who run the Aboriginal pathway. I'm glad the process was more about who I am as a person and the capacity I have, rather than who I am on a piece of paper.

REVIEWS

☺ 'Pay is very competitive for a graduate salary.'

☺ 'I've enjoyed working on meaningful programs and projects that I can see have a positive impact on the community. Even as a grad, I feel I've been able to make a valuable contribution.'

Read the full interview and more reviews at 🚀 **au.prosple.com**

#96

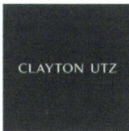
CLAYTON UTZ

Clayton Utz

`3.8` ★★★★☆

#4 in Law

LEARN MORE AND APPLY NOW!
———
scan to visit their profile

Accepting applications from*	L
Types of opportunities	Graduate jobs Clerkships
Location of opportunities	⊙ Sydney, Melbourne, Brisbane, Perth, Canberra

WHAT IT'S LIKE?

Olivia Barns
Lawyer

Having a workplace with a diversity of culture, experience or thought can only be a good thing as it means you can always learn from someone who sees things differently.

REVIEWS

☺ 'Balance of decent pay and work/life balance + culture.'

☺ 'The people make coming to work every day enjoyable.'

Read the full interview and more reviews at 🚀 **au.prosple.com**

---

key for degrees where they accept applications from on page 7

#97 GSK

GSK
4.5 ★★★★½
#1 in Pharmaceuticals

Accepting applications from* B C E H I L M P S T

Types of opportunities Graduate jobs Internships

Location of opportunities ⊙ Melbourne, Sydney, Auckland

WHAT IT'S LIKE?

We want GSK to be a place where people feel inspired, encouraged and challenged to be the best they can be. A place where they can be themselves – feel welcome, valued and included. Where they can keep growing and look after their wellbeing.

REVIEWS

☺ 'Supportive team, flexible working hours, wealth of knowledge, ongoing training, satisfaction of working with candidate and hiring managers, building relationships and networking.'

☺ 'They are accessible and approachable, and they have mentored me in different ways.'

Read the full interview and more reviews at 🚀 **au.prosple.com**

#98 CSL

CSL
4.2 ★★★★☆
#2 in Pharmaceuticals

Accepting applications from* B E M S

Types of opportunities Graduate jobs Internships

Location of opportunities ⊙ Melbourne

WHAT IT'S LIKE?

Mitch Winzer
Risk & Vulnerability Sourcing Specialist – Global Direct Materials

My global role allows me to work with new people from all around the business and the world every day on a wide range of different activities, keeping the job interesting. Getting to travel abroad with work is pretty exciting, too!

REVIEWS

☺ 'Very good salary for a graduate.'

☺ 'Very casual, fairly flat structure. Everyone wants to support each other. The culture is very friendly and open.'

Read the full interview and more reviews at 🚀 **au.prosple.com**

*key for degrees where they accept applications from on page 7

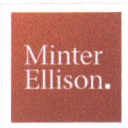

#99 MinterEllison

4.3 ★★★★☆
#5 in Law

Accepting applications from*   B C E H I L M P S T

Types of opportunities   Graduate jobs   Clerkships

Location of opportunities   ⦿ Sydney, Melbourne, Canberra, Darwin, Perth, Brisbane, Adelaide, work from home

WHAT IT'S LIKE?

Emily Hill
Lawyer

I get to work on exciting, challenging and high profile legal matters where I can learn from specialised lawyers who are experts in their chosen field, in an environment where I genuinely enjoy coming to work, feel comfortable being myself and have fun. To me, MinterEllison's emphasis on positive growth and learning is invaluable.

REVIEWS

☺ 'The workplace culture is fantastic. As a junior, it feels like everybody genuinely cares about your development and interests.'

☺ 'There is a huge emphasis on diverse recruitment and opportunities.'

Read the full interview and more reviews at 🚀 **au.prosple.com**

#100 FTI Consulting

4.2 ★★★★☆
#12 in Accounting & advisory

Accepting applications from*   B E H I L P S T

Types of opportunities   Graduate jobs   Internships

Location of opportunities   ⦿ Sydney, Brisbane, Melbourne, Perth

WHAT IT'S LIKE?

Charlotte Stocks
Assistant, Corporate Marketing

The best thing about my job is that no two days are the same – it's such a dynamic environment. I love that every day I face different challenges and new learning curves that help me to grow and develop as a professional... I've never felt more welcome and comfortable in a professional environment. My colleagues are so supportive and eager to help out...

REVIEWS

☺ 'I genuinely really like everyone that I work with. They are great colleagues.'

☺ 'Very ethnically diverse workforce, with employees with cultural backgrounds from all across the globe. The firm is very committed to employing women in both senior positions and grad positions.'

Read the full interview and more reviews at 🚀 **au.prosple.com**

key for degrees where they accept applications from on page 7

prosple

Career Ambassador

Share your story & inspire futures!

Help millions of students by sharing your real-life career experience.

Scan to know more